The Theory of Imperfect Competition

A RADICAL RECONSTRUCTION

COLUMBIA STUDIES IN ECONOMICS

2

THE THEORY OF

Imperfect Competition

 A RADICAL

RECONSTRUCTION

by Donald Dewey

New York and London · *1969*

COLUMBIA UNIVERSITY PRESS

Donald Dewey is Professor of Economics
at Columbia University.

Copyright © 1969 Columbia University Press
Library of Congress Catalog Card Number: 73-79190
Printed in the United States of America

Preface

The skeptical reader who is faced with yet another book on imperfect competition is entitled to expect from the author a word of explanation and very possibly an apology. I respectfully submit three justifications for venturing to presume on the reader's patience. The first can be advanced by any reasonably conscientious scholar who has pursued his calling for twenty years. I believe that I have learned a few truths and perfected a few pedagogical artifices that may interest fellow specialists. The second justification is more substantial. There exists a *prima facie* case that the theory of imperfect competition—and by imperfect competition is meant all forms of competition that are not "perfect"—ought to be restated in the interests of greater rigor, clarity, and relevance to the policy problems of market regulation. Indeed one can properly question whether the rambling, eclectic treatment in the typical textbook or treatise on oligopoly, product differences, mergers, cartels, spatial competition, price discrimination, etc., should even be described as *the* theory of imperfect competition. Such a treatment has none of the coherence of the treatment of perfect competition and, on this score, seldom compares favorably with the original work of Joan Robinson. There is, I submit, a strong presumption that somebody's restatement of the theory of imperfect competition will ultimately advance the cause of economics.

However, it is the third justification for offering this book to which I attach the most weight. During most of my life in economics I have had the good fortune to contend with both the venerable issues of axiomatic economic theory and the disordered subject matter of industrial organization. No doubt this sort of incomplete specialization has its drawbacks; it certainly increases the labor cost of keeping up with the relevant work of one's colleagues. But it does have the advantage of exposing the practitioner to a continuing collision of perspectives that often produces a nagging doubt and sometimes an arresting idea. I would cite two examples of the benefits of incomplete specialization from personal experience.

A long immersion in the issues of abstract capital theory first led me to suspect that most of the empirical work on the nature of unit cost functions in the firm was mostly worthless simply because any cost function constructed from accounting data inevitably contained an element of rent. And the inclusion of this element will change both the location and the shape of the empirical unit cost function over any given range of output. However, it was time spent with the musty records of the *United States Industrial Commission* (1899–1904) that first caused me to doubt that an "equilibrium with firms of less than optimum size" could long endure in a model that stipulated freedom of contract. The records clearly revealed that, in the real world, J. B. Duke and other promoters had become exceedingly adept, while American antitrust policy was nonexistent or in its infancy, at rationalizing whole industries with the aid of mergers, cartels, and spinoffs.

I hasten to add that both of these "discoveries" were original only in the sense that they are not yet to be counted among the propositions whose validity most economists with a recent graduate training take for granted. Martin Bronfenbrenner demonstrated in 1950, in a neglected article, how monopoly profit is transmuted into cost by the capitalization process, while M. A. Copeland had assumed in 1934, as a matter of course, that the then emerging theory of imperfect competition was not relevant to the activities of the multiplant firm.

Over the years, as I worked both in axiomatic economic theory and with the refractory details of industrial organization, two suspicions gradually hardened into convictions. The first has been suggested above. I came to believe that the bits and pieces of theorizing about oligopoly, mergers, spin-offs, product differences, spatial competition, etc., could be arranged in a pattern that would constitute a unified theory of imperfect competition. (One may greatly admire the complicated universe of imperfect polypoly, pliopoly, oligopoly, etc., that Professor Fritz Machlup has given us and still feel that it condemns economics to more disorder than is necessary or profitable.) I also came to believe that many of the things which economists seek to do with the partial equilibrium theory of perfect competition could better be done with a unified theory of imperfect competition. It is, of course, for the reader to judge whether this book assembles the evidence needed to justify either or both of these convictions.

For all defects of workmanship in the attempted reconstruction I must accept sole responsibility. Still, author, if not reader, can take comfort in the certain knowledge that the task would have been far worse done without the help of fellow workers. My debts are especially heavy to William Geoffrey Shepherd, who politely but firmly exposed the unreadiness of an early draft, and William Vickrey, who expended a part of his hard-earned leave time on an exceptionally troublesome chapter. I would also like to thank the following colleagues who read and criticized parts of the manuscript at one stage or another:

Roger Alcaly, Gary Becker, Richard Brief, David Chessler, Harold Demsetz, Alfred Eichner, Albert Hart, Charles Issawi, Kenneth Jones, Jacob Mincer, and Charles Shami.

Donald Dewey

New York City
November 1, 1968

A NOTE ON TERMINOLOGY

With not a few misgivings I finally decided to call this book *The Theory of Imperfect Competition: A Radical Reconstruction.* A more accurate title would be *Another Look at the Theory of Imperfect and/or Monopolistic Competition and Oligopoly with Some Attention to Policy Implications and the Methodology of Economic Models.* But, of course, not even a university press will stand for such a title these days. Two features of my choice of terms deserve an explanation.

My decision to speak throughout this book of imperfect competition with virtually no reference to monopolistic competition, save in Chapter 5, is dictated mainly, but not entirely, by the desire to keep to a standard terminology. This usage also accords with a belief that, as far as methodology goes, this book is closer to Joan Robinson than to Edward Chamberlin. This presumed affinity in no way implies a denigration of Chamberlin's achievement, even though, in common with most economists of the present day, I can no longer grant his claim that monopolistic competition is a unique economic phenomenon. I do believe that work in Chamberlin's tradition is more difficult to assimilate into axiomatic economic theory than is work in the Robinson tradition. But I believe that the difficulty of assimilating the Chamberlin approach can be taken as conclusive evidence that, when the object is to understand how competition works in the real world, axiomatic economic theory is not enough.

I have also chosen to call this book a radical reconstruction rather than a restatement or a new exposition. This choice of words is intended to indicate the limits of my presumption. On the one hand, I firmly believe that, where the theory of imperfect competition is concerned, *mere* revision no longer will suffice. The errors and ambiguities are, I believe, serious enough to make advisable not merely a refurbishing and updating of Robinson and Chamberlin but a rebuilding effort that will radically change the use made of the theory of imperfect competition. On the other hand, I am under no illusion that this effort at reconstruction exhibits that "flash of genius" once so highly valued (and seldom found) by federal courts in patent litigation. If it is judged by the reader to constitute a useful, if pedestrian, advance on the prior art, I shall be satisfied. In fact, almost all the features of this book which have some claim to novelty have pedigrees that are both ancient and honorable. They mostly embody ideas, like the limit or stay-out price or the inherent instability of oligopoly as a form of market organization, that, for one reason or another, have never gained a well-defined place in axiomatic economic theory.

Contents

The Theory of Imperfect Competition

A RADICAL RECONSTRUCTION

The very forest of man's thoughts chokes up his thoroughfare. A man must be orthodox upon most things, or he will never even have time to preach his own heresy. G. K. CHESTERTON

CHAPTER 1 *The Case for Change*

1 · SOME DIFFICULTIES OF DEFINITION. The principal object of modern economics is the study of competition: how it works in the real world; how it would work if economic institutions were changed; and how it works in models that economists construct in order better to understand the real world. Unhappily, as economists and people who deal with economists know to their sorrow, no simple all-purpose definition of competition is possible; indeed, in a modern economy that makes extensive use of markets and an elaborate division of labor, the term competition is virtually a synonym for "economic activity." However, four features of competition are explicitly or implicitly stressed by virtually all definitions.

First, competition embodies the process of free exchange whereby one trader persuades others to comply with his wishes by offering them a service or commodity in return—or the money with which to buy it. We note that nothing need be said about the equity of free exchange. The process can involve a transaction wherein a starving man trades his father's watch for a loaf of bread, or one wherein one party cruelly misrepresents the character of the good or service that he offers. Free exchange is free only in the limited sense that no force or intimidation is used by either side, the negations of free exchange being robbery, blackmail, threats against life and property, and, in the case of government versus citizen, expropriation of property or forced labor. The idea of free exchange also implies the existence of what is usually termed free entry; that is, established producers have no legal right to bar aspiring competitors from entering the industry.

Second, almost every definition of competition has connotations of "rivalry" (the conspicuous exception being, of course, the definition of perfect competition). Sellers of a product are presumed by unilateral action to seek to advance their own interests at the expense of sellers of the same or similar products. The forms of business rivalry defy enumeration, but the most common are, as we know, price cutting, advertising, and product improvement. Rivalry is merely another name for "incomplete collusion" and hence always exists to the extent that sellers fail to behave "as if" they were employees of the same firm.

We note that the concept of rivalry also implies the existence of economically interesting alternatives. Every trader in the market is presumed to have both the opportunity to choose the parties with whom he will deal and an incentive to deal with some parties in preference to others. Unhappily, this feature of competition is never precisely delineated because the cost of discovering customers and suppliers differs vastly from one market situation to another. (In models of perfect competition, economists sidestep this complication by assuming that the cost of securing market information is zero, that it is a matter of chance which seller deals with which buyer.) When we say that an industry is "highly competitive," we mean that the cost of locating another customer or supplier is negligible. If I do not like the coffee served by restaurant A, I can get a cup from restaurant B by walking a few yards. Or I can take my chances with the office vending machine. Likewise, when we say that an industry is "not very competitive," we mean that the cost of locating an alternative customer or supplier is so high relative to the gain promised by the contact that few traders make the effort. One deals with the local insurance agent in a small town simply because it would be too costly in time and effort to visit nearby towns in the hope of finding a more satisfactory agent.

Third, every definition of competition explicitly or implicitly assumes that some part of the behavior of individuals and business firms in the market place is predictable. In a private enterprise economy, predictability is presumed to be provided by the ubiquity of avarice: by the assumptions that, *ceteris paribus,* every seller prefers a higher price to a lower price and every buyer prefers a lower price to a higher price. In the case of a socialist economy that seeks to use competition as an organizing principle, predictability is secured by directing the state-owned firms to behave "as if" they were income maximizers. It is hardly necessary to observe that, in both private enterprise and socialist economic systems, income-maximizing behavior by firms is subject to a large number of constraints.

Fourth, every definition of competition explicitly or implicitly assumes that some part of the behavior of individuals and business firms in the market place *is not* predictable. Innumerable economic decisions are made under conditions that involve uncertainty. Hence some fraction of the economic behavior described as "competitive" consists of actions which are exploratory in the sense that they are employed in order to secure information that the manager hopes will have a payoff that exceeds its cost of collection. For example, when a new product is introduced, the firm has need of information on the prices at which different quantities can be sold, and the obvious way to secure it is to experiment with different prices and to tabulate and analyze the sales results.

In this connection we ought to emphasize that it is highly misleading to view the search phase of an economic activity as the short interval of time that precedes a settling into some static phase. Exploratory behavior is a permanent feature of competition as the term is understood by everyone (including the economist whenever he talks about real-world competition). In order to depict more clearly certain features of the competitive process (most notably how resources are moved from one industry to another as their owners seek maximum returns), economists often use the concept of competitive equilibrium in which, *inter alia,* all producers and consumers have complete information on everything relevant to their economic decisions. But real-world competition is strictly a phenomenon of disequilibrium; in fact, it disappears as the conditions necessary for "competitive equilibrium" are approached.

We could continue to list the connotations of "competition" *ad infinitum,* but such dedication would carry us into negative net returns very quickly. Enough has been said to indicate that, to most of us, competition denotes both a state and a process. Or, more precisely, it denotes many states and many processes. For example, it can signify a state in which the industry consists of two or more firms or one wherein price is approximately equal to long-run marginal cost of production. Likewise the term can signify a process by which the entry or exit of firms brings price closer to long-run marginal cost, or one by which the economic system or the industry itself creates the disturbances in the form of new products and new machines that keep the industry from ever closing this gap.

That competition as a process *may* destroy competition as a state is true by definition, since process is movement from one state to another. That competition as a process *will* destroy competition as a state unless the industry is buffeted by exogenous shocks that preserve disequilibrium is perhaps not so obvious. (In Chapter 9 we make use of recent developments in formal information theory to offer a formal proof of the last proposition.) For present purposes it will suffice to make the mental note that alerts us to the verbal pitfalls that threaten whenever we speak of "competition" or "the competitive process." The many unique and subtle connotations of the terms make it unthinkable that we should try to operate without them. Unhappily, these varied connotations also ensure that we shall have some difficulty in operating with them.[1]

2 · SOME DOCTRINAL HISTORY. For many years after economics emerged in the early 1800s as a formal discipline of study, economists made no special effort to define

---

[1] In the great majority of cases the statement "competition has decreased in industry X" will have much the same meaning for the speaker and his audience. Both will interpret it to mean that the number of important firms has declined, price changes are becoming less frequent, and the products of the surviving firms are more standardized.

Nevertheless, there are instances when such a message would be given diametrically opposed interpretations by speaker and audience. One such case is provided by product differences that have their origins in an antitrust rule. If economies are to be had by standardizing products, and an industry is not yet in equilibrium, the member firms will through mergers and cartels, seek to secure these economies by reducing product differences. By one verbal usage, an antitrust rule which blocks this adjustment is "anticompetitive" because it thwarts a more efficient use of resources. By another usage, such a rule preserves competition because it preserves product variety for consumers. In this case effective communication between speaker and audience unavoidably requires the use of a more elaborate vocabulary. The difficulties of deciding whether product differences make for more or less competition are examined in Hans Brems, "Cartels and Competition," *Weltwirtschaftliches Archiv*, LXVI (1951), 51–69.

competition. In common with everyone else, they simply assumed that competition was the higgling and, bargaining of the
market place. They felt no compelling need to distinguish the
different varieties of competition. Indeed, we have it on the
authority of Professor Stigler,[2] who has searched the old books,
that the concept of competition did not begin to receive explicit and systematic attention until the 1870s when the major
works of W. S. Jevons [3] and J. E. Cairnes [4] appeared. By his
reckoning the first attempt at a rigorous definition of perfect
competition—the concept that is the principal cutting tool of
modern economic theory—was not made until the appearance
of F. Y. Edgeworth's *Mathematical Psychics* (London, 1881).

An intriguing question is: Why did economists in the latter
years of the nineteenth century fail to develop an explicit theory
of imperfect competition at the time they were constructing the
explicit theory of perfect competition? Several circumstances
seem to have combined to produce this neglect. One is that,
while competition can be perfect in only one way, it can be
imperfect in innumerable ways; hence innumerable theories of
imperfect competition are possible. Again, the construction of
a model of imperfect competition is inherently a more difficult
task than the construction of a model of perfect competition;
and it is plausible that older economists did not view the intellectual payoff to be had by going beyond perfect competition
to be worth the effort. One bit of evidence for this view is the
fact that the great treatise writers of the past, notably J. S. Mill,
Alfred Marshall, Frank Taussig, Herbert Davenport, and F. M.
Taylor, either ignored the pioneer work of Augustin Cournot

[2] G. J. Stigler, *Essays in the History of Economics* (Chicago, 1965),
pp. 239–44.

[3] *Theory of Political Economy* (London, 1871).

[4] *Some Leading Principles of Political Economy Newly Expounded*
(London, 1874).

and F. Y. Edgeworth on the classic duopoly problem of economics or treated it as an intellectual curiosity that had very little significance for the everyday business of life.

But the main reason why the formal study of imperfect competition was neglected by older economists is simply that they felt no need for it. They might accept that perfect competition in the real world was an impossibility; but until well into the twentieth century most economists did not doubt that, in the long run and in the absence of government restraints on freedom of contract, the prices of goods and services in the real world were determined in essentially the same way as in a model of perfect competition. Insofar as the imperfections of competition were studied by economists, they were regarded as irritating frictions, temporary impediments to the achievement of competitive equilibrium that were destined by pass away.

Actually there were good reasons why older economists were reluctant to become enmeshed in the methodological problems of defining competition. Although they clearly perceived that no industry in the real world could be perfectly competitive, their main concern was with competition in the real world rather than the problems of methodology in economics. So long as no formal definition of competition was insisted upon, they could discuss those features of real-world markets (including their imperfections) which they regarded as significant; and they could organize the discussions as they pleased. The model of a perfectly competitive market could be introduced whenever it could usefully illuminate some important feature of reality. It could be laid aside whenever it got in the way of the study of other important features of reality.

Thus the older approach to competition tended to be discursive rather than axiomatic, and it characterized every influential treatise on economics in the English-speaking world before the discovery of F. M. Taylor's *Principles*.[5] This discursive approach to competition has never been wholly abandoned by British economists. In the United States, however, the rise of specialized graduate training favored the cause of self-conscious abstractions; so that by the 1920s, the study of economic theory had come to be the study of the perfectly competitive model with ever less attention being given to its uses for illuminating reality. The preoccupation with methodology that overtook American economists in the 1920s is well illustrated by the most influential textbook of the decade—F. M. Taylor's *Principles*—which is surely the most demanding introduction to the subject ever inflicted upon college sophomores. For Taylor is concerned almost entirely with production and distribution in a perfectly competitive model. The real world receives only perfunctory mention, and the theory of monopoly is disposed of in less than five pages. If, as Professor Samuelson contends, much of the work of economists in the years from 1920 to 1933 "was merely the negative task of getting Marshall out of the way," [6] the highest prize for ground clearing in the United States belongs to Taylor.

In the fascinating and much neglected *Synthetic Economics* (1929), H. L. Moore went beyond Taylor by declining even to mention the possible imperfections of competition. Whenever Moore writes "competition" the reader must read perfect competition. The truth would seem to be that, while economists were slow to embark upon self-conscious theorizing about competition, the task of constructing the partial equilib-

---

[5] Taylor's *Principles of Economics* did not receive widespread attention until 1921 when its copyright was taken over by Ronald Press. Some of the chapters on money were published by a local printer in Ann Arbor for Taylor's students as early as 1906.

[6] P. A. Samuelson, "The Monopolistic Competition Revolution Revisited," in *Monopolistic Competition Theory: Studies in Impact,* R. E. Kuenne, editor (New York, 1967), p. 111.

rium theory of perfect competition was completed in fairly short order in the years 1900–1920. The capstone was Frank Knight's *Risk, Uncertainty and Profit* (1921); its discussion of the methodological problems involved in defining perfect competition has never been surpassed. Thus Joseph Schumpeter could write, in 1930, on the eve of the Robinson-Chamberlin revolution, that:

Some ten or twenty years ago, the state of Economic Theory was somewhat analogous to what it was during the quarter of a century which followed upon the publication of Mill's *Principles*. To a superficial observer at least, there seemed to be a tendency among many of the most competent economists to accept as "final" the fundamentals, or more than fundamentals, of our theoretical apparatus, to discourage further investigation into its time-honoured problems, and to consider further refinements as superfluous or worse . . . There was a belief that the great work had been done —a belief very similar to that expressed by Mill in that famous passage, which winds up his exposition of the theory of value, viz., that there was nothing left to clear up "either for the present or any other writer." [7]

For better or worse, when the partial equilibrium theory of perfect competition had been perfected, only a limited number of things could be done with it. One could continue to use it in the Marshall-Taussig manner, that is, to cast light on competition in the real world while taking care to point out how the assumptions of the model differed from the facts of business life. As a second possibility, one could relegate the theory of perfect competition to the status of a curiosity in the history of economic ideas, as some of the so-called institutional economists recommended during the 1920s. Finally, one could seek to supplement, or possibly replace, the theory of perfect

[7] The quotation is from Schumpeter's preface to F. Zeuthen, *Problems of Monopoly and Economic Warfare* (London, 1930), p. vii.

competition with other types of axiomatic price theory. In the 1920s there was already precedent for this third approach, for the body of axiomatic price theory even then included a complete theory of monopoly and at least three solutions to the duopoly problem first propounded by Cournot.

Whatever the merits of these three possible reactions to the appearance of the formal theory of perfect competition, the greatest influence has been wielded by economists who sought to supplement or replace it with other types of axiomatic price theory. While the list of economists who have made valuable contributions in this work over the last thirty-five years is long indeed, the great names are, of course, Edward Chamberlin and Joan Robinson.

3 · THE ACHIEVEMENT OF ROBINSON AND CHAMBERLIN. With the omniscience of the backward glance we know now that the emergence of a subdiscipline in economics labeled "the theory of imperfect competition," or some similar title, represented far less of a break with tradition than many economists of the 1930s supposed. (American economists seem to have been especially gullible in ascribing originality to the new ideas; Mrs. Robinson, after all, was quite careful to acknowledge her intellectual debts.) The appearance of the books of Robinson and Chamberlin did, however, radically recast the teaching of economics and encourage a very great number of empirical studies of competition. If the results of this research have been disappointing (and they have given rise to few truths important enough to include in a basic economics course), the impact of Robinson and Chamberlin on the teaching of economics has nevertheless been permanent. Three factors probably explain most of their collective pedagogical impact.

The first was the chance circumstance that their books appeared together, so to speak, out of the blue. They arrived within six months of each other and with almost no advance warning in the form of previously published journal articles or notes containing much the same material. As a result, critics fell rapidly to comparing their differences and similarities and debating the significance of their common contribution to formal economic theory. A second and much more important factor in the Robinson-Chamberlin success story was the quality of the achievement. *The Economics of Imperfect Competition* and *The Theory of Monopolistic Competition* not only contained much that was new; the major arguments were so carefully developed and forcefully presented that almost none of the novelty was lost through inept exposition.

Economists can reasonably debate which of the several innovations in economic theory introduced by Robinson and Chamberlin deserves to rank as the most original. But a perusal of any sample of economics textbooks or treatises published since 1933 leaves no doubt about the most influential of their innovations. They were their explicit introduction into economic theory of the premise that the firm faces a negatively inclined demand curve for its product, and their demonstration that, when this is done, marginal revenue perforce diverges from average revenue.[8] Nowadays a textbook or treatise writer in economics need not bother to mention the importance that Chamberlin attached to product differences as a method of

[8] Fritz Machlup, *The Economics of Sellers' Competition: Model Analysis of Sellers' Conduct* (Baltimore, 1952), pp. 150–52; W. S. Vickrey, *Microstatics* (New York, 1964), pp. 314–22; R. G. Lipsey and P. O. Steiner, *Economics* (New York, 1966), pp. 313–17; K. J. Cohen and R. M. Cyert, *Theory of the Firm: Resource Allocation in a Market Economy* (Englewood Cliffs, N.J., 1965), pp. 207–28; C. E. Ferguson, *Microeconomic Theory* (Homewood, Ill., 1966, pp. 251–66.

competition or Robinson's remarks on the exploitation of labor, but he cannot fail to recapitulate their treatment of the firm's negatively inclined demand curve. For Robinson and Chamberlin demonstrated to the satisfaction of virtually everyone that the behavior of the firm in an imperfectly competitive market could be succinctly described with the aid of their geometry; and that such a description was more elegant and pedagogically more efficient than the previous practice of expounding the theory of perfect competition and then appending a few observations on how the model diverged from the real world.

The books of Robinson and Chamberlin did, of course, much more than introduce and popularize the marginal revenue function which had long led a shadowy existence in the theory of demand. Robinson's discussion of price discrimination broke new ground, and Chamberlin's insistence upon the importance of product differences directed attention to a market phenomenon that had previously received little systematic attention. Add also that much of the modern work on the theory of oligopoly seems to have descended directly from Chamberlin's reconsideration of the venerable duopoly problem.

There is one further reason why the *Economics of Imperfect Competition* and *The Theory of Monopolistic Competition* were so avidly read and discussed when they first appeared. Both were published in the worst year of the Great Depression in the United States, and, by arguing that a policy of laissez-faire did not, even in a simple economic model, produce optimum results, they provided ammunition to the many economists who not unreasonably had come to believe that existing economic institutions were in need of drastic revision. Thus the Robinson-Chamberlin achievement became "not only a legitimate analytical framework but also a device for dramatizing in an exaggerated way at least some of the sins of capitalism." [9] The fact that neither book in any way implied that laissez-faire was responsible for mass unemployment was conveniently forgotten. It was enough that both books seemed to indicate that, *ceteris paribus,* laissez-faire leads to technically inefficient production and a maldistribution of resources. This demonstration also provided ammunition to more than one set of critics of the status quo. It was useful to socialists who hoped to increase economic welfare by resort to planning; it was just as useful to liberals who hoped to increase economic welfare by devising and enforcing stricter antitrust laws.

Whatever the reasons that explain their astounding success thirty-five years ago, the books of Robinson and Chamberlin ensured that henceforth formal theorizing about the behavior of the firm would not be confined to the polar cases of monopoly and perfect competition. An explicit theory of imperfect competition was here to stay, even though it would not always be a Robinson or Chamberlin version. This obvious truth would not be worth mentioning were it not that, in recent years, not a few economists who should have known better have, in deprecating the achievement of Robinson and Chamberlin, in effect, argued for a return to the pre-1933 treatment of competition.[10] The case for turning the clock back is made to

[9] R. L. Bishop, "The Theory of Imperfect Competition after Thirty Years: The Impact on General Theory," *American Economic Review,* LIV (May, 1964), 37.

[10] The most intemperate objections to the theory of imperfect competition have come from economists who, while students or young teachers at the University of Chicago, learned their economic theory and much of their scientific methodology from Frank Knight. See, for example, G. J. Stigler, "Monopolistic Competition in Retrospect," in *Five Lectures on Economic Problems* (London, 1949), pp. 12–24; or Milton Friedman, "The Methodology of Positive Economics," in *Essays in Positive Economics* (Chicago, 1953), pp. 38–39. For Chamberlin's reply to his harshest critics, see his essay on "The Chicago School," in *Towards a More General Theory of Value* (New York, 1957), pp.

rest upon both an ideological and a pedagogical objection to the theory of imperfect competition. The ideological objection is that the theory of imperfect competition, as expounded in the classroom, creates a "bad" image of capitalism while the theory of perfect competition creates a "good" image. This objection is not without substance, but it relates to the partisan uses which are made of the theory and not to its intrinsic merits and hence need not be discussed in this book.

The pedagogical objection to the theory of imperfect competition takes two forms. The first alleges that the theory is superfluous—it does not allow us to discover any important truth about the real world that cannot be discovered with the aid of a model of perfect competition. In this form the objection is either wrong or tautological.[11] (It is merely tautologi-

296–306. A reasonably dispassionate survey of the issues is found in G. C. Archibald, "Chamberlin versus Chicago," *Review of Economic Studies,* XXIX, 1 (1961), 2–28.

[11] As a nearly self-evident example of an important truth that *cannot* be established without the aid of the theory of imperfect competition, I offer the following. It is really a fastidious formulation of the much discussed excess capacity theorem of Robinson and Chamberlin that we shall meet later on.

Assume that every plant in an industry has a fixed cost in the short run; that neither economies nor diseconomies are to be had from multiplant ownership; and that entry into the industry is free. Then a legal rule which restricts the number of plants that can be placed under common ownership will bring about an equilibrium characterized by excess capacity; that is, in equilibrium, the industry will be producing an output which could be obtained more cheaply if some plants were closed and the remaining plants were operated at a level which minimizes unit cost of production. A proof for this theorem is developed in Chapter 4.

If the industry is presumed to be perfectly competitive, the preceding conclusion does not follow. Rather the conclusion must be that a legal rule which restricts plant ownership has no economic effects whatsoever. (For the present we pass over the possibility that the assumption that each plant has a fixed cost may be incompatible with the assumption that the industry is perfectly competitive.)

cal if the important truths about the real world are implicitly defined as those which can be discovered with the aid of a model of perfect competition.) The second form of the pedagogical objection says, in effect, that the theory of imperfect competition directs the student's attention to the wrong things; that it causes him to concentrate on the imperfections of competition when, in the interest of understanding how competition works, he should be learning how mentally to discount these imperfections. The appropriate answer to this form of the pedagogical objection is that, since every market in the real world is imperfectly competitive, economists must perforce say something about imperfect competition. The choice is between the *ad hoc* treatments of the subject in the years before 1933 (see almost any chapter in the books of Alfred Marshall or Frank Taussig) and the axiomatic treatment of imperfect competition opened up by Robinson and Chamberlin. The case for an axiomatic treatment of perfect competition is that it permits us to perceive clearly certain relationships that would otherwise go unnoted or unappreciated. The case for an axiomatic treatment of imperfect competition is, of course, precisely the same.[12]

[12] We cannot do better than leave the final word in defense of the theory of imperfect competition to Professor Samuelson: "To reject, as I was taught to do in Chicago, monopolistic competition on the ground that it is not a 'nice, simple, unified' theory like that of perfect competition is like insisting that $f(S') \equiv 0$ because that is simpler and more manageable. If perfect competition is the best simple theory in town, that is no excuse for saying we should regard it as good theory if it is not good theory . . . We must not impose a regularity—or approximate regularity—in the complex facts which is not there. Good science discerns regularities and simplicities that are there in reality—I almost said 'out there.'" *The Collected Scientific Papers of Paul Samuelson* (Cambridge, 1966), II, pp. 1777–78.

evidence that this form of competition is a product of the American antitrust laws that restrict mergers and outlaw cartels, and that, in the absence of this legislation, oligopoly would rapidly give way to monopoly or, at any rate, to something that looks like monopoly. Of course, nobody seriously supposes that in the near future the American economy is going to relax the restraints that it has imposed on mergers and cartels. But so great a part of economic analysis is grounded on the assumption of free exchange that economists are duty-bound to consider the results competition would produce in the total absence of these restraints.

Third, most treatments of the theory of imperfect competition either baldly assert or plainly imply that imperfect competition is economically wasteful; that is, they contain some version of the so-called "excess capacity theorem." They argue that economic waste results because the organization of production is technically inefficient: each plant will operate at an output where its average total (or unit) cost is falling, and there is the additional danger that the plant itself will be of less-than-optimum size. They argue that economic waste also results because imperfect competition causes price to exceed marginal cost and so reduces economic welfare. A few economists, however, have always been reluctant to base judgments about the imperfect competition of the real world upon the inferences that can be drawn from studying the operation of the economic model of imperfect competition.[15] In this reluctance

[15] Such skepticism is apparent in virtually every chapter of J. M. Clark's, *Competition as a Dynamic Process* (Washington, 1961). A certain caution about inferring economic waste from the existence of a negatively sloped demand curve for the firm is also apparent in Chamberlin himself. Indeed, one of Chamberlin's students has even argued that his contention that the tangency solution implies economic waste was not meant to apply to the case where sellers are so numerous that each ignores the possibility that his own actions may

they seem instinctively to have perceived a truth that we shall develop explicitly and at length in the pages that follow: the model itself is unsatisfactory.

Fourth, in the more sophisticated treatments of imperfect competition the notion of a "limit" or "stay-out" price has long led a shadowy existence. That is, many writers have drawn the obvious inference that, if entry into an industry is possible, any sensible firm will take into account how far its price-output policy operates to make the industry attractive to potential competitors. But these writers have not followed through by outlining a stay-out pricing strategy for an established firm because to do so is a very tedious operation. (It involves, for example, scrapping the simple rule that a firm produces the output at which marginal cost is equal to marginal revenue.)

Fifth, the all-important process of joint maximization, wherein rival firms combine and cooperate to increase profits, has been neglected in treatments of imperfect competition. This neglect seems to have occurred mainly because the most common instrument for securing joint maximization is the cartel— a business arrangement which has long been outlawed or regarded with deep suspicion in most English-speaking countries. In fact, in the United States even the attempt to form a cartel has been a penitentiary offense since the Addyston Pipe case (1899).[16] Nevertheless, all theorizing about the nature of competition should begin with the assumption that every kind of cartel is legal. Such an assumption is implicit in any type of economic theory which gives the owners of resources "freedom of contract." Moreover, it is naive to suppose that the process of joint maximization can be obliterated by outlawing the cartel;

affect the actions of the others. J. M. Cassels, "Excess Capacity and Monopolistic Competition," *Quarterly Journal of Economics,* 51 (1937), 435–37.

[16] *Addyston Pipe & Steel Co. vs. United States,* 175 U.S. 211 (1899).

the goal, after all, can be pursued by methods which are not illegal, most notably mergers, subcontracting, and the mental telepathy of oligopolists. If this book has a claim to a unifying theme, it is the conviction that the theory of imperfect competition should be rebuilt to take explicit account of roles played by stay-out pricing and joint maximization of profits.

Sixth, the distinction that economists often draw between "statics" and "dynamics" has been cavalierly treated in the theory of imperfect competition with results productive of much avoidable confusion and terminological quibbling. The failure to observe the distinction can, I think, be traced to the lack of interest of Robinson and Chamberlin in problems of methodology and to the strong policy orientation of many later students of the subject. Certain theorems in the theory of imperfect competition require the assumption that all producers act with complete information while other theorems require the contrary. Thus the theorem which states that, given complete freedom of contract (and hence the right to form a profit-sharing cartel), rival producers will never engage one another in economic warfare requires the former premise and is invalid on the latter premise. (The conditions which give rise to economic warfare are considered in some detail in Chapters 6 and 7.)

Another result of the failure to observe the distinction between statics and dynamics is a persisting confusion about the role of information in competition. *A priori,* economists have every reason to believe that an increase in the amount of information available to producers and consumers will have some consequences for competition. As yet they have not been carefully spelled out. At one extreme we have the often-cited implication of Chamberlin's work that, if an increase in information deprives the producers of power to vend a differentiated product, movement will be in the direction of perfect competition.[17] At the other extreme is the not-so-well-known conjecture of Frank Knight that, if the spread of information reduces the uncertainty associated with the investment decision, movement will be in the direction of "monopoly." [18] In the middle range we have J. M. Clark's surmise that socially acceptable forms of competition require the availability of certain kinds of market information and the absence of other kinds.[19]

Since competition has more facets than any one writer can ever hope to identify, it is too much to expect that we shall ever be able to state the last word on how an increase in information will affect competition. Still, we can reasonably hope to increase our own information about the problem.

Seventh, the loose ends of the controversy touched off by Chamberlin's analysis of product differences are still with us. My own feeling is that the typical textbook or treatise discussion of the subject is unsatisfactory in three important respects. It fails to set forth clearly the criteria used to distinguish between good and bad product differences. It does not relate the

[17] *The Theory of Monopolistic Competition,* especially Appendix E, "Some Arguments in Favor of Trade Mark Infringement and 'Unfair' Trading," pp. 271–74. Here Chamberlin argues that a weakening of trademark protection will increase competition by standardizing products in ways that consumers can perceive clearly and distinctly.

[18] "With perfect intercommunication it would seem that the assumed absence of collusion is very improbable, as organization costs would naturally tend to a low level. Under static conditions (with the existing stocks of all agencies fixed and known), a great development of monopoly would apparently be inevitable. It is not unreasonable to suppose even that in the absence of organized social interference conditions would approach the result contended for by the Marxian socialists, monopoly universal, or at least prevalent to an extent involving the complete breakdown of the competitive system of organization." *Risk, Uncertainty and Profit* (Boston, 1921), p. 190.

[19] *Competition,* especially Chapter 19, "Common Requirements of Healthy Competition," pp. 465–90.

amount of product differentiation practiced by the firm to the costs that must be incurred to differentiate some "basic" product. Finally, it errs in attributing excess capacity to excessive product differentiation, whereas, in fact, excess capacity will not characterize equilibrium unless some artificial restriction has been placed upon size of firm. If such a restriction exists, the excess capacity that results may well be associated with a certain amount of product differentiation. But the latter in no sense "causes" the former. Indeed, it is entirely possible that a constraint that reduces firm size may result in the industry having too little product differentiation when judged by some acceptable test of economic welfare. The precise impact upon product differentiation of a restriction on firm size will depend upon the cost functions which govern the process of producing and differentiating a product.

Yet here, again, it will be found, I think, that, when the returns are in, the results of our investigation will prove to be neither outstandingly original nor disturbingly heretical. The typical textbook or treatise discussion of product differences may leave much to be desired. But when one turns to the vast literature on the subject to be found in academic journals and industry trade publications, it is reasonable to assume that every significant result has been anticipated by somebody's accurate observation and/or careful theorizing.

5 · A FINAL ARGUMENT FOR INTELLECTUAL RE-VISIONISM. In conclusion, we may cite the general argument for revisionist efforts in scientific work. It has been elegantly put by Professor George Stigler.

A new idea does not come forth in its mature scientific form. It contains logical ambiguities or errors; the evidence on which it rests is incomplete or indecisive; and its domain of application is exaggerated in certain directions and overlooked in others. These deficiencies are gradually diminished by a peculiar scientific ageing process, which consists in having the theory "worked over" from many directions by many men. This process of scientific fermentation can be speeded up, and it has speeded up in the modern age of innumerable economists. But even today it takes a considerable amount of time, and when the rate of output of original work gets too large, theories are not properly aged. They are rejected without extracting their residue of truth, or they are accepted before their content is tidied up and their range of applicability ascertained with tolerable correctness. A cumulative slovenliness results, and is not likely to be eliminated until a more quiescent period allows a full resumption of the ageing process.[20]

Only two observations need be added. The turbulence of the times into which the theory of imperfect competition was born was especially calculated to foster the "cumulative slovenliness" which Stigler fears. Moreover, decay as well as progress is possible in the treatment of any scientific idea, since information, like capital equipment, has a cost of maintenance. Indeed, it seems to be the rule that, once textbooks begin to recapitulate the treatment of any subject in which sustained research has largely ceased, the deterioration begins. The reason is probably that, when a subject ceases to be fashionable, textbook writers lose interest in the qualifications that the authors of the original research attached to their work. With an author's presumption, I hope that this book will represent a visible improvement in the theory of imperfect competition. But I shall count it a worthwhile failure if it merely retards the intellectual decay that causes textbook and treatise writers to equate the theory of imperfect competition with a perfunctory description of a few diagrams taken from two books published in 1933.

[20] Stigler, *Essays*, p. 14.

CHAPTER 2 *The* *Tangency*
Solutions

1 · SOME CONVENTIONAL GEOMETRY. Let us begin by restating the theory of imperfect competition as it is found in most modern textbooks and treatises on economic theory. This is a rather tricky undertaking because the various treatments differ in extent of coverage and place of emphasis. However, they all have one thing in common: the geometry of the tangency solution first popularized by Robinson and Chamberlin. That is, these treatments all incorporate a diagram which shows a firm producing an output where a falling curve of unit cost is tangent to the firm's demand curve and a rising marginal cost curve intersects a falling marginal revenue curve (Figure 2-1).

In most treatments of imperfect competition it is either explicitly stated or plainly implied that the tangency solution is dictated by the premise of "free entry," that is, by the assumption that no legal, institutional, or technological barrier prevents new firms from entering the industry. Hence, whenever an industry becomes profitable, new firms will enter and expand its output; and the influx of new firms will continue until all profit has been squeezed out of the industry and the incentive to enter has been eliminated.

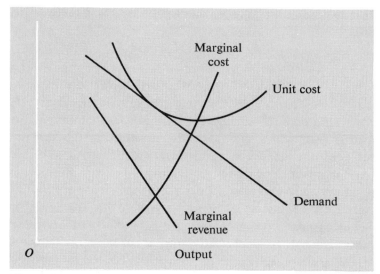

Figure 2-1

As usually interpreted, the tangency solution is held to indicate that, in equilibrium, the imperfectly competitive industry is technically inefficient in that the equilibrium output could
be more cheaply produced if distributed among a smaller number of firms.[1] Often it is also implied that economic welfare is
reduced under conditions of imperfect competition in the sense
that too little output is produced by the industry. Among the
welfare critics of imperfect competition, there is, however, no
agreement on the rule which should be followed for raising output, though one widely accepted rule would have it increase

[1] See, for example, Fritz Machlup, *The Economics of Sellers' Competi-
tion: Model Analysis of Sellers' Conduct* (Baltimore, 1952), pp. 306–08;
P. A. Samuelson, *Economics: An Introductory Analysis* (New York,
3rd ed., 1955), pp. 460–72; R. G. Lipsey and P. O. Steiner, *Economics*
(New York, 1966), pp. 313–17; or K. J. Cohen and R. M. Cyert,
Theory of the Firm (Englewood Cliffs, N.J., 1965), pp. 207–26.

until the industry's long-run marginal cost becomes equal to price.[2]

2 · A FUNDAMENTAL AMBIGUITY. We can immediately discern a disconcerting ambiguity in the usual textbook description of equilibrium in imperfect competition. No specific instructions are given for constructing the demand curve of the imperfect competitor. Presumably it is some function of the demand for the industry's product. But how it is drawn must also depend upon how the rivals of the imperfect competitor are assumed to react to his alterations of output. Standard treatments of imperfect competition are either silent on this point or uncomfortably vague. A very great number of assumptions about the behavior of rivals is possible. Each one is, in some respects, "unrealistic" since real-world behavior always involves a certain amount of experimental activity and "learning by doing" which cannot be completely described. Nor can this difficulty be resolved by saying that each firm assumes that its own price-output decisions have no effect on the outputs of other firms. In this situation, if the firm is presumed to have perfect knowledge of the demand for the industry's product, then it regards the "unused" portion of the industry demand curve as its own. If the firm is presumed not to have this perfect knowledge, then its own demand curve becomes an entrepreneurial guess which need bear no fixed relation to the unused portion of the industry's demand curve.

Actually, there is no such thing as *the* tangency solution in the theory of imperfect competition. Innumerable possibilities

[2] The search for the best rule for allocating resources is surveyed in I. M. D. Little, *A Critique of Welfare Economics* (Oxford, 2nd ed., 1957), pp. 129–65; and E. J. Mishan, *Welfare Economics: Five Introductory Essays* (New York, 1964), pp. 155–83.

exist because, as we shall presently see, each assumption about how rival firms react to one another's changes in output dictates a different tangency solution. In this respect the problem of finding equilibrium in imperfect competition is analogous to the problem of finding equilibrium in the classic duopoly case of economic theory. We cannot pause here to identify any great number of the many tangency solutions that are possible. Therefore let us concentrate on two extreme cases which, for ready identification, we shall call solution A and solution B.

3 · TANGENCY SOLUTION A: THE FOLLOW-ANY-LEADER CASE.

In the first instance let us assume that all firms have identical production functions; that any change in output of the individual firm will immediately be matched by all of its rivals; and hence that the output of the industry will always be divided equally among the firms that comprise it. On these assumptions we can without difficulty relate the equilibrium output of the firm to the equilibrium output of the industry.

Let curve DD' in Figure 2-2 be the demand curve for the industry's product. If the industry consists of two firms, each has the demand curve DM (whose slope is twice that of curve DD' in the figure). If the industry consists of four firms, each has the demand curve DN (whose slope is four times that of curve DD' in the figure).

In a no-profit-no-loss equilibrium consisting of n firms the demand curve of each firm has a slope equal to n times the slope of the industry's demand curve. When $n = 4$, Figure 2-3a depicts equilibrium price and output for the single firm and Figure 2-3b depicts equilibrium price and output for the whole industry. Thus the output OX in Figure 2-3b is equal to four times the output OC in Figure 2-3a.

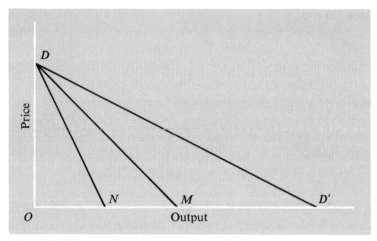

Figure 2-2

Note that Figures 2-3a and 2-3b denote an equilibrium in two restricted meanings of the term: none of the four firms already established in the industry has an incentive to expand output; no fifth firm has an incentive to enter the industry. If it did enter (and the market continued to be divided equally among all producers), it would face a demand curve with five times the slope of curve DD' in Figure 2-2, that is, a demand curve that was below the firm's curve of unit cost at every level of output.

We might note parenthetically that the unique assumption underlying tangency solution A—the premise that any change in the output of the individual firm will immediately be matched by all its rivals—is one of the more plausible possibilities. In fact, it is almost always explicitly or implicitly used by economists who seek to explain price-output decisions in industries where sellers are few, their respective shares of the market are relatively constant over time, and price changes are relatively infrequent.

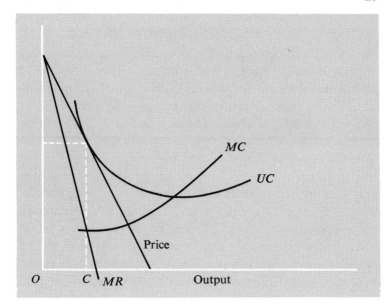

Figure 2-3a

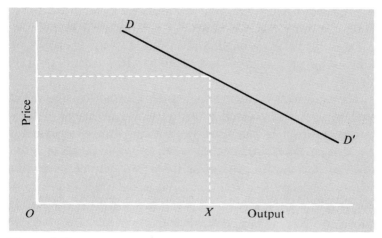

Figure 2-3b

4 · TANGENCY SOLUTION B: THE COURNOT-TYPE
CASE. In deriving tangency solution A we assumed that
any output change by one firm is immediately matched by all
other firms with the result that the market is always equally divided among them. When sellers are few—say two, three, or
four—this premise of equal division is plausible. After all, in
many industries with but a few sellers, market shares of the leading firms are remarkably constant over time. However, the preceding analysis also implies that, the greater the number of firms
in an industry, the more inelastic is the demand facing each individual producer at a given output. And for many economists
this conclusion is too unorthodox to be swallowed. For to the
extent that they learn the fundamentals of their trade by ex-
amining models of perfect competition, economists come to assume that, *ceteris paribus,* the more firms in an industry, the
more closely it approximates pure competition. Hence, the more
firms in the industry, the more elastic is the demand for a given
output in the single firm. Therefore, with a bow to Augustin
Cournot, let us now posit that in planning its output each firm
always assumes that the output of its rivals will remain unchanged; that this assumption is, in fact, "wrong"; but that no
firm ever manages to discover through experience that it is
wrong.

The derivation of equilibrium in this Cournot-type case is a
tedious process.[3] However, we may legitimately ignore it, since
the truth which is important for our purposes was long ago
made clear by Cournot: on the above assumptions, the individual firm always behaves as if its own demand curve has

[3] For the mechanics of getting to equilibrium under Cournot's assumptions, see his *Recherches sur les principes mathématiques de la
theorie des richesses* (Paris, 1838); Edward Chamberlin, *The Theory of
Monopolistic Competition* (8th ed., 1962), pp. 30–35; or Machlup,
Sellers' Competition, pp. 368–77.

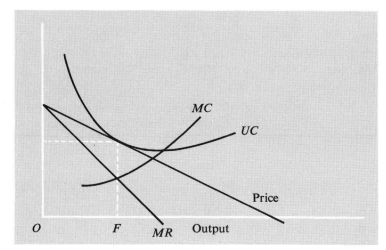

Figure 2-4a

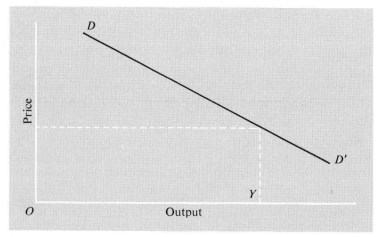

Figure 2-4b

the same slope as that of the industry's demand curve. Hence in equilibrium the firm will produce the output at which the slope of the curve of unit cost is equal to the slope of the industry's demand curve.

Equipped with this knowledge, we can directly determine tangency solution B. Equilibrium price and output for the firm are given by Figure 2-4a, and equilibrium price and output for the industry are given by Figure 2-4b. The number of firms that tangency solution A supports in equilibrium is equal to the integer obtained by dividing output OF in Figure 2-4a into output OY in Figure 2-4b. In this example the equilibrium number of firms is three.[4]

5 · TANGENCY SOLUTIONS A AND B COMPARED.
Here we might pause to compare the results of tangency solutions A and B. We note first that solution B gives the lower equilibrium price and higher equilibrium output for the industry. We note also that there is less technical inefficiency in solution B since each firm produces at a lower point on its curve of unit cost. No matter how we write down our cost and revenue functions, we shall always have these differences between solutions A and B. In our examples, tangency solution B supports three firms and solution A supports four firms. Given the conventional geometry of price theory, solution A must have at least as many firms as solution B. One cannot obtain

---

[4] Following the venerable tradition that has come down undisturbed from Robinson and Chamberlin, Figures 2-4a and 2-4b are tailored to ensure that all profit in the industry is eliminated when exactly three firms occupy the industry. This result can be secured only by a careful selection of cost and revenue functions. If we begin with a demand function for the industry and a cost function for the firm chosen at random, equilibrium will almost certainly be reached with each firm earning some positive profit (or rent) which, however, is not large enough to attract an additional firm into the industry. The conventional geometry is retained here because it allows us to avoid the troublesome but not very important issue: How is the unit cost curve to be drawn when the firm in equilibrium earns a permanent profit (or rent)? That is, should we treat such a return as a surplus above unit cost or a part of unit cost?

the contrary result without positing a demand curve for the industry for which the price elasticity of demand rises as price falls.

We might pause again to remind ourselves that tangency solutions A and B are but two of many possible equilibria for an industry in imperfect competition. Every rule that prescribes the behavior of the imperfect competitor in the face of uncertainty about how his rivals will behave dictates its own unique equilibrium. However, we are entitled to believe that certain of these rules are inherently more reasonable than others. It makes little sense to posit that the firm behaves "as if" the demand for its output is perfectly elastic or, to go to the other extreme, to posit that the firm believes that a 10 per cent increase in its own output will be matched by a 20 per cent increase in the output of every rival. The rules that underlie tangency solution A and tangency solution B have the merit of establishing the upper and lower bounds of plausible behavior. That is, it is surely reasonable to believe that every entrepreneur will consider that his share of the market will be no less than his share of the industry's plant capacity; and that he will consider that the demand for his own output at any price cannot be greater than demand for the industry's output at the same price. On these assumptions, in a no-profit-no-loss equilibrium the industry's output must be at least as great as output in solution A but no greater than output in solution B.

6 · CHAMBERLIN ON TANGENCY. Since the geometry of our tangency solutions A and B has some novelty, it seems advisable to relate it to the familiar geometry of Chamberlin.[5] We shall not pause to relate it to the equally familiar

---

[5] *Monopolistic Competition*, pp. 90–92.

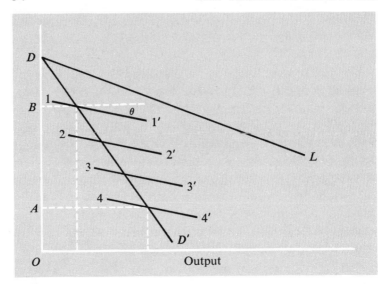

Figure 2-5

but less elaborate geometry of Robinson. For reasons that are mainly of interest to specialists in the history of economic ideas, Chamberlin chose to derive his tangency solution on the assumptions that the "industry" consists of a large group of firms which produce different varieties of the "product," and that each member firm produces a single, unique variant of this product.

Consider Figure 2-5. Line *DL* gives the quantity demanded for all varieties of the product at various prices. (If the product is "fresh fruit," *DL* perforce sums up apples, oranges, etc.) Line *DD'* is the demand curve for the variety of product produced by one producer drawn on the assumption that "his competitors' prices are always identical with his." In Chamberlin's large-group case (so-called to distinguish it from his discussion of oligopoly) the single producer is presumed not to know—and never to learn from experience—that a price cut on his own variety will be matched by his rivals. Thus, should price stand at *OB*, he believes that the demand curve for his variant of the product is given by line 1-1′; thus, if the marginal revenue implied by this imaginary demand curve is above his marginal cost, he will expand output.

However, Chamberlin's producer is mistaken: his price cuts will be matched by his rivals who produce other variants of the product. Therefore, as all firms, acting simultaneously or in sequence, increase output, the imaginary demand curve of the producer in Figure 2-5 slides down *DD′*. When price has fallen to *OA*, the producer believes that this demand curve is 4-4′. Note that a postulate of product variety is necessary to give a negative slope to lines 1-1′, 2-2′, etc. If the product is homogeneous, the producer will behave as if he faced a perfectly elastic demand for his variant of the product and lines 1-1′, 2-2′, etc., would be horizontal. Thus in Figure 2-5 the angle θ serves as an index of the "degree of product differentiation."

Chamberlin's long-run equilibrium is described by Figure

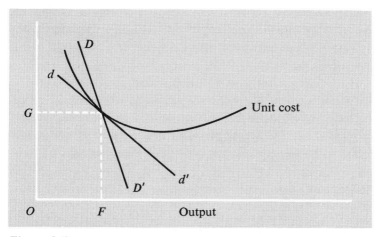

Figure 2-6

2-6, surely one of the most famous geometrical constructions in the history of economics. When this equilibrium has been achieved, two results are visible. The imaginary demand curve *dd'* is tangent to the curve of unit cost; and the point of tangency is intersected by *DD'*. Now the firm has no incentive to change its price *OG,* since marginal cost is equal to marginal revenue; and, since price is equal to unit cost, *DD'* will not be shifted to the left by the entry of new firms nor to the right by the exit of established firms. Actually, the last conclusion depends upon Chamberlin's heroic premise that, although rival firms produce differentiated products, they all have identically shaped curves of unit cost and hence Figures 2-5 and 2-6 stand for all firms in the large group.

The geometry needed to deal with the case of firms which produce different varieties of the product is decidedly more cumbersome than that which suffices for the case of a homogeneous product. For example, in Figure 2-5 line *DL* is not a constant but rather depends upon the number of different variants of the product that are produced. As additional firms producing additional variants enter the group, *DL* shifts upward. As this happens, the intercept of *DD'* with the price axis moves upward while its intercept with the quantity axis moves to the left.

How does the entry of new firms producing new variants of the product affect the slopes of the imaginary demand curves 1-1', 2-2', etc.? Provided that we adhere strictly to Chamberlin's assumption that each producer believes that a price reduction will go unmatched, the answer is clear enough.[6] *Ceteris*

[6] We could use a more sophisticated economic model than did Chamberlin—one in which, for a producer of a differentiated product, the probability that a 5 per cent price cut will increase sales by X amount is an increasing function of the number of firms in his group. In such a model the slopes of the imaginary demand curves 1-1', 2-2', etc., may increase, decrease, or remain unchanged as the number of

paribus, consumers in general prefer more product variety to less, and the individual consumer prefers a more differentiated product to a less differentiated one. Therefore, as product variety expands, it becomes more difficult for the producer of brand Y, for example, to increase output sold by a 5 per cent price cut. The slopes of the curves 1-1', 2-2', etc., must become steeper as the entry of new firms adds to product variety.

Fortunately, it will not be necessary for us to appraise Chamberlin's geometry in any great detail. Our main concern is with price making under conditions of imperfect competition and not with the economic consequences of product differentiation. Given this orientation, there is no need to forgo the gain in clarity and elegance to be had by positing an industry that consists of firms that produce a homogeneous product. In any event, we argue in Chapter 5, where product differences are considered, that they can be more efficiently handled with simple algebra and calculus than with elaborate geometry.

7 · NUMBER OF FIRMS AND TANGENCY. We have already asserted that, while innumerable tangency solutions are possible, none is plausible which yields an equilibrium output greater than that of solution B. In order to get a greater equilibrium output, the producer must believe that, if he increases his own output by, say, 10 units, his rivals will react by actually cutting their aggregate output by, say, 8 units. The assumption that a producer believes that an increase in his output will be accompanied by a decrease in the aggregate output of his rivals is not really inconsistent with any of our other assumptions. It represents a logical possibility. But since it is even

firms and product variety increase together. On the difficulty of generalizing about the connection between product variety and competition, see Machlup, *Sellers' Competition,* pp. 161–66.

more unrealistic than Cournot's assumption that a seller always treats the outputs of his rivals as fixed, there is no point in making use of it.

There is, of course, a basis for believing that a real-world industry can be made "more competitive" by increasing the number of firms. However, this is so only because no seller in the real world ever has the complete information on prices that static theory assumes. In the real world, to increase the number of firms is to raise the cost of securing such information and hence to encourage an entrepreneur to believe that his variations in price or output will go undetected, at least for a time, by some rivals.[7]

Economists sometimes seem to imply that, as market information becomes more complete in an industry, the industry becomes more competitive. Since "competitive" is an adjective with many connotations, one is reluctant to say that this implication is wrong; but it can be misleading. Most of the confusion about the connection between number of firms and the intensity of competition can be traced to the failure to keep firmly in mind the distinction between a perfectly competitive market and a merely perfect market.[8] All static theory assumes the existence of the perfect market which, by definition, is one wherein arbitrage is so effective that equal units of the same product sell for the same price. This is so whether the subject of study is perfect competition, imperfect competition, monopoly, or oligopoly. Any development which brings about a costless increase in market information available to buyers and sellers in the real world helps to "perfect the market" by lowering shopping and selling costs. However, the effect of such a

[7] For one of the few studies of the role of information in a market see G. J. Stigler, "The Economics of Information," *The Journal of Political Economy,* LXIX (1961), 213–25.

[8] On this truth see G. J. Stigler, *Essays in the History of Economics* (Chicago, 1965), pp. 244–45.

development on the number of firms is uncertain (if only because it depends partly upon the elasticity of demand for the industry's product). And the effect of an informational improvement associated with a change in the number of firms upon the behavior of individual firms is even more difficult to ascertain. Whether a decline in the number of firms, if it occurs, should be equated with a "decline in competition" is a question that we postpone until Chapter 4.

8 · THE LIMITED VALIDITY OF TANGENCY SOLUTIONS. Since the whole theory of imperfect competition that has come down from Robinson and Chamberlin rests upon the tangency solution, it is well that its ambiguous character should be identified and, if possible, dispelled. Nevertheless, as far as the cardinal thesis of this book is concerned, the discussion of tangency is merely ground clearing for the main event. One hesitates to say that the solutions A and B that we have just described are "wrong." We can say categorically, however, that both solutions are incompatible with the assumptions that economists usually make in economic theory. More specifically, an organization of production that is technically inefficient cannot be a stable equilibrium provided that the following conditions are present:

Technology and access to factor markets are open to all actual and prospective producers on equal terms.

The owners of productive factors have complete freedom of contract in selling or renting them out.

Over some range of output, the costs of bringing plants under a common central management are zero or null.

All firms are profit maximizers.

In Chapter 4 we shall demonstrate that, on these assumptions, any tangency solution, if it should ever exist, must give way to a permanent equilibrium in which production is efficiently organized (in the sense that there is no cheaper way of producing whatever output is produced). There we shall see that this "true" equilibrium output is always less than the output implied by tangency solution B. It may be equal to, greater than, or less than the output implied by tangency solution A.

It remains for us now only to speculate on why so little attention has been paid over the years to so important a crack in the foundation of the Robinson-Chamberlin achievement. One possible answer, distinctly unflattering to economists, was suggested in the last chapter: the will to believe was simply too strong. The tangency solution is, on its face, an indictment of laissez-faire (if only a small one), and the noble idea of contractual freedom has, of course, been under attack from different sections of the political spectrum for many years. However, an answer more charitable to economists can also be brought forward. Impressed and possibly shaken by Chamberlin's claim that the theory of monopolistic competition was something radically new under the sun, they failed to see that there was no necessary connection between his geometry and his sophisticated verbal discussion of advertising, selling costs, product differentiation, and oligopoly.

To obtain a stable tangency solution there must be some obstacle to combining firms under a common central management. At first glance it seems possible that an obstacle is posed by the fact that, in Chamberlin's world, an industry consists of firms that produce different, though similar, products. Actually, the existence of different products does not bar the achievement of technically efficient production, but the proof of this proposition entails some rather fastidious theorizing. It seems best to delay it until Chapter 5, when we have accomplished the easier task of showing that, given freedom of contract, the tangency solution is unstable when the industry is defined as the set of firms selling the "same" product in the "same" market.

CHAPTER 3 *A Geometry of*
Multiplant Operations

1 · SOME USEFUL TOOLS. Later in our analysis of imperfect competition we shall have occasion to use a number of ideas that are either not mentioned or lightly treated in most discussions of the subject. Of these ideas the most important is what older economists and businessmen often called by the name "rationalization of industry," the most conspicuous tools of rationalization being cartels, mergers, gentlemen's agreements, and subcontracting. Since the major goal of rationalization is the more efficient use of plant capacity, let us begin with the neglected geometry of multiplant operations.[1]

We note immediately that, in generalizing about these operations, a certain caution is in order, because the smooth cost functions of the economics textbooks and treatises cannot be used to describe the cost situation of the multiplant firm. It has the option of operating all its plants or only some of them; and the cost of producing any given output will be affected by the number of plants in which the output is produced. In the multi-

---

[1] See, however, Don Patinkin, "Multi-Plant Firms, Cartels, and Imperfect Competition," *Quarterly Journal of Economics,* LXI (1947), 173–80; and William Fellner, *Competition among the Few* (New York, 1949), p. 202.

plant firm, only the fraction of costs which are by definition "fixed" is independent of the number of plants used to produce a given output. And since, in the short run, fixed costs do not influence the price-output decision of the firm, let us derive first the multiplant firm's curve of average variable cost. We shall limit our attention to the case where there are no "front office" costs that need to be considered, that is, no costs incurred by non-manufacturing divisions that must be arbitrarily imputed to the outputs of the several plants of the firm. The technique employed to allocate front office costs is rather involved; and the inclusion of such costs in our analysis would not change it in any significant respect, since the cost of producing any given output would still be affected by the number of plants used to produce it.[2]

We can begin by distinguishing the two types of variable cost functions that are possible for multiplant firms. The first occurs when we assume that average variable cost in each plant increases with output beginning with the first unit produced. The second occurs when we assume that average variable cost decreases in each plant for a time as output expands. (In this second case the curve of average variable cost has the U-shape found in most textbooks.) In each plant, average variable cost must, of course, eventually rise as output expands, since an average variable cost that declines continuously with output contradicts the law of variable proportions.[3]

---

[2] The problem of allocating front office costs is considered in Martin Shubik, "Incentives, Decentralized Control, the Assignment of Joint Costs and Internal Pricing," in *Management Controls: New Directions in Basic Research*, C. P. Bonini et al., editors (New York, 1964), pp. 205–26.

[3] When the multiplant firm distributes a given output among its plant so as to minimize average variable cost, it also minimizes the unit cost of that output (which is, of course, the sum of average variable cost and average fixed cost). However, it is more convenient to con-

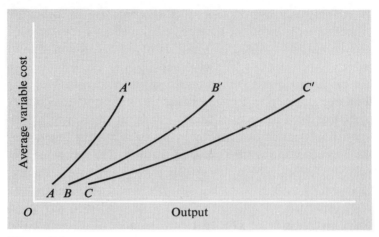

Figure 3-1

Figure 3-1 depicts the first type of variable cost function for a firm with three identical plants. If the firm should choose to operate only one of its three plants, its curve of average variable cost is AA'. If the firm should choose to operate two of its three plants, it will divide output in a way that keeps marginal cost equal in both plants; that is, it will divide output equally between them since the two plants are identical. When two plants are operated, average variable cost is given by BB' in Figure 3-1. Finally, should the firm choose to operate all three plants, it will divide output into three equal parts and its curve of average variable cost will be given by CC' in Figure 3-1.

duct our analysis in terms of average variable cost. The allocation of total fixed cost among the plants of the multiplant firm is arbitrary; and, when one plant is closed in the course of a rationalization scheme, the amount of the firm's total fixed cost previously allocated to it must now be divided among the plants that remain in operation. Thus average variable cost in a single plant depends only upon the quantity of output produced in it, whereas average fixed cost and hence unit cost in the plant depend upon the number of plants in the firm that are operated.

The case where average variable cost increases in the plant, beginning with the first unit of output produced, is neither very important nor very interesting. It is a safe assumption that, in most situations, the economies to be had by setting up a division of labor in the plant ensure that the curve of average variable cost is approximately U-shaped. In situations where the geometry of Figure 3-1 applies, the only economically significant curve is CC'. For if the curve of average variable cost rises continuously in each plant—and all plants are equally efficient—our multiplant firm, if it operates at all, will always use all three plants.

The more interesting case where, in each plant, the curve of average variable cost is approximately U-shaped is shown by Figure 3-2. Here again we posit a firm with three identical plants. Curve AA' is again a curve of average variable cost drawn on the assumption that all of the firm's output is pro-

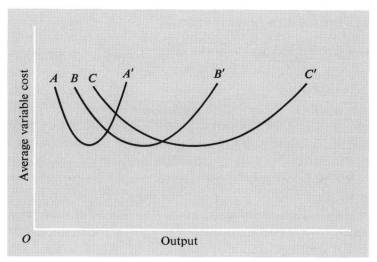

Figure 3-2

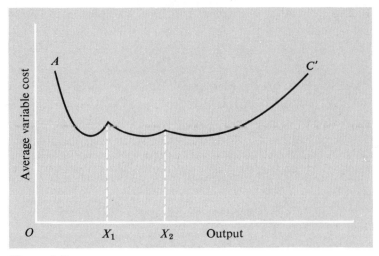

Figure 3-3

duced in one plant while the other two plants are closed. Curve *AA'*, being the conventional curve of average variable cost which is found in most textbooks on economic theory, presents no problems. If the firm elects to operate two of its three plants, the total variable cost of any given output is minimized by dividing it equally between the two plants. On the assumption that two plants operate, the firm's curve of average variable cost is *BB'* in Figure 3-2. If the firm elects to operate all three plants, output will, of course, be divided equally among them, and the relevant curve of average variable cost becomes *CC'* in Figure 3-2.

We perceive that, for all rates of output except three, the three-plant firm of Figure 3-2 has three possible figures for average variable cost, and that only the lowest of these three figures is relevant in making the price-output decision. The "true" curve of average variable cost for the three-plant firm is given by curve *AC'* in Figure 3-3. It indicates that, for rates

industry that completely satisfies all the require-
erfect competition.) Before this change was wrought
Nature, the following conditions prevailed:
plants of all firms had been equally efficient at any
t.

iction in the industry was carried on under condi-
pproximately constant returns to scale. That is, re-
ale were constant in the restricted sense that the in-
tput could be increased without any rise in unit cost
additional plants and assigning each plant a produc-
that minimizes unit cost.

mplify the analysis we shall further assume that one
nt is superior to all others irrespective of its planned
d hence that no problem is involved in choosing the
size" plant.

industry was in long-run competitive equilibrium in
or each firm, price was approximately equal to unit
) each plant had produced that output at which unit
owest.

demand for the industry's product is "given."

we have said nothing about the number of plants
y each firm. Provided that there are neither econo-
iseconomies of management, in the proximate case
competition the number of plants that each firm will
indeterminate but unimportant. As long as entry into
y is free, the number of plants per firm does not
equilibrium price and output of the industry.

t pause to emphasize that the existence of long-run
e equilibrium implies the possibility of instantaneous
the industry. For if the members of the industry can
to restrict output and raise price without immediately
the entry of new firms, they will always do so. This
hat they will always tacitly collude or enter into a

of outputs less than OX_1, one plant will be operated. For rates
of outputs greater than OX_1 but less than OX_2, two plants will
be operated. And, for rates of outputs greater than OX_2, all
three plants will see service. At an output of exactly OX_1 the
firm is indifferent between operating one or two plants; at an
output of exactly OX_2 the firm is indifferent between operating
two or three plants.

Our technique of constructing the curve of average variable
cost can easily be generalized to include the case of the n-plant
firm whose plants are of unequal efficiencies. The multiplant
firm will, to repeat, always operate that number of plants which
will allow it to minimize the total variable cost of a given output. This means that, *in those plants that it operates,* marginal
cost will everywhere be equal.

Once we have derived the curve of average variable cost for

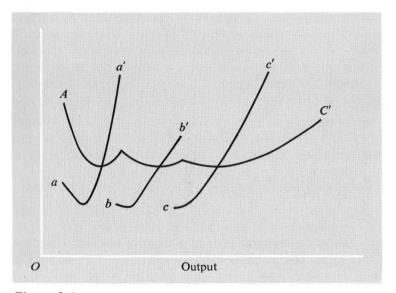

Figure 3-4

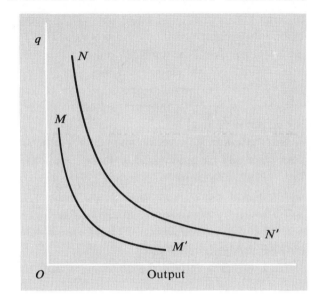

Figure 3-5

the multiplant firm, it is an easy task to derive the relevant curves of unit (or average total) cost and marginal cost. Since the curve of average variable cost is kinked (the kink occurring whenever an additional plant is brought into production as output expands), the curve of unit cost is also kinked; and the marginal cost curve is discontinuous. In Figure 3-4 the relevant marginal cost curves for our three-plant firm (aa', bb', and cc') have been imposed on the curve of average variable cost taken from Figure 3-3.

The geometry of the multiplant firm is completed by Figures 3-5 and 3-6. In Figure 3-5 curve MM' gives average fixed cost for the single plant while NN' gives average fixed cost for the firm that has constructed three plants. When NN' in Figure 3-5 is added to AC' in Figure 3-3, the curve of average variable cost, the result is a curve of unit cost for the three-plant firm. Unit cost is depicted in Figure 3-6.

2 · A TRANSITION TO

kinked curves of unit
a discontinuous marginal c
look at a most venerable pr
tion of price and output und

Let us start with the cas
the assumption of industr
gangsters or possibly a n
policy, has made it impossit
what had previously been a
competitive industry. (We h
inevitability of fixed costs i

Figure 3-6

thing as
ments of
by Man c

1. The
given out

2. Pro
tions of a
turns to s
dustry's o
by buildir
tion quot:

3. To
type of pl
output, a
"optimum

4. The
that (a)
cost and
cost was

5. The
As yet
operated
mies nor
of perfect
operate is
the indus
affect the

We mi
competiti
entry into
cooperate
provoking
is to say

short-run cartel agreement. (We return to this truth in Chapter 6.)

Once the natural catastrophe or change in government policy has erected an absolute barrier to the entry of new firms—and always assuming that the state imposes no antitrust type restrictions on freedom of contract—the perpetuation of competition by the members of the industry becomes irrational conduct. "Obviously" the industry can be most profitably operated as a technically efficient monopoly, and only two problems arise. How rapidly shall the industry move from competitive equilibrium to monopoly equilibrium? What administrative arrangements will allow this adjustment to be made at the lowest possible cost?

The movement to monopoly equilibrium will, of course, involve the shutting down of some plants whenever there are more than a handful of plants in the industry. Let us assume that in competitive equilibrium the industry had consisted of six plants. If we make the convenient assumption that the industry's demand curve is linear (nothing is gained by assuming that it is not linear), three of these plants must be shut down if monopoly profit is to be maximized. In Figure 3-7, let the output in competitive equilibrium be given by the distance OT. At this output, price is equal to both marginal cost and unit cost; and unit cost is minimized. (Only a fragment of the unit cost curve is shown in Figure 3-7 since unit cost is not relevant to the price-output decision in the short run.) When the monopolist takes over, he maximizes profit by cutting back to output OS where marginal cost is equal to marginal revenue.

It is somewhat surprising to find that the monopolist has an incentive to discontinue production in three plants "immediately," that is, as soon as he has received, from the state or Nature, a grant of protection against the entry of all newcomers. The fact that the plants chosen for closing may be

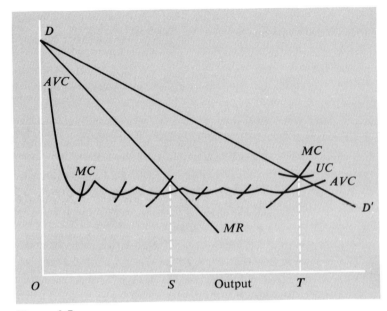

Figure 3-7

"brand new" is not significant. Fixed cost does not affect the price-output decision; hence the efficiency of the three plants shut down has nothing to do with the rate at which output is cut back.

If all plants are indestructible and can last forever, the closed plants are simply scrapped or sold for whatever they may bring. On the more plausible assumption that plants wear out with use, the three plants closed down will presumably be put into the industrial equivalent of mothballs for some period of time. They will be returned to production as the three plants that remain in operation wear out. If it is possible eventually to "use up" three plants, unit cost falls as the number of plants in existence declines from six to three. However, this downward shift in the location of the unit cost curve does not affect the marginal cost of producing the profit-maximizing output; hence it does not affect the size of the rationalized industry's output.

Let us turn now to the second problem confronting the members of an industry who have been presented with the golden opportunity to monopolize. What administrative arrangements will allow the movement from competition to monopoly to be made at the lowest possible cost?

Probably the most obvious organizational possibility is the profit-sharing cartel. Three plants are chosen for closing. The net revenue obtained from producing OS (Figure 3-7) in the other three plants that continue to operate is equal to

Total revenue less (i) the total variable cost of producing OS (including an allowance for wear-and-tear depreciation on the three plants operated) and (ii) the cost (if any) of maintaining the three closed plants on a standby basis.

This net revenue is the monopoly profit which is to be divided among the fortunate owners of the industry; and, since all plants are identical, they will divide it according to the fraction of output which each owner produced in the old competitive equilibrium.

3 · CARTEL ALLOCATION OF OUTPUT QUOTAS. In the cartels of the real world there is often a great deal of hard bargaining over the assignment of output quotas and the division of profits. However, on the assumptions of this chapter that demand for the industry's product is given, that technological developments can be foreseen, and that the exclusion of new firms is permanent, there is no scope for bargaining over

output quotas. For an equal division of the net receipts of an output of *OS* (Figure 3-7) produced in three plants makes every owner better off and, perforce, no owner worse off. Should any owner be offered less than an equal share of the net receipts of output *OS,* he can increase his profit by withholding part of his cooperation and so reduce the net receipts available for division among the others.

We can assume that initially each of the six plant owners receives a quota that allows him to produce one-sixth of output *OS* in Figure 3-7. But clearly, in a world of free contract, every quota owner will make one of two moves. Either he will seek to buy another quota so that he can operate his plant at a lower average variable cost or he will seek to sell his quota to someone who will produce in this way. In order to introduce bargaining over quotas or profit shares into the picture, we must assume that different entrepreneurs have different tastes for business independence. This possibility we have ruled out.

4 · OLIGOPOLY VERSUS MONOPOLY. Here we might digress to note that the foregoing analysis of how monopoly will come to the multiplant industry after it is closed to newcomers has a number of interesting and neglected implications for public policies toward merger and oligopoly. Consider the proposition often advanced by critics of antitrust that "from the standpoint of consumers there is little to choose between oligopolistic price policies and those of a monopolist." [4]

Proponents of this view argue, in effect, that, when an industry consists of a very small number of firms, the members can achieve, by a sort of mental telepathy, the same restriction

[4] G. W. Stocking and M. W. Watkins, *Monopoly and Free Enterprise* (New York, 1951), pp. 90–91.

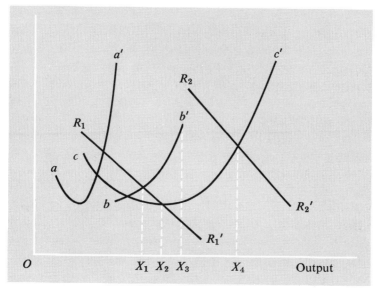

Figure 3-8

of output that would result if they were placed under a unified central management. The disturbing implication of this view is, of course, that the efforts of American antitrust are a waste of time to the degree that a policy of trust-busting and blocking mergers merely replaces the obvious monopoly of the single firm with the sluggish competition of the few. Happily, we can demonstrate that, whatever the defects of antitrust may be, this alleged inadequacy is not one of them.

Figure 3-8 depicts the marginal cost curves of an industry consisting of three identical plants on the assumption that it can be organized in two different ways. (We continue to assume that new firms are effectively barred by Man or Nature from the industry.) If the industry is operated as a multiplant monopoly, the marginal cost curve of the monopolist is given by the set of discontinuous curves in Figure 3-8. (Recall that discontinuity is implied by the monopolist's power to open and close plants.) If the industry consists of three plants operated by three independent oligopolists who are precluded by law, custom, or shortsighted suspicion from sharing profits, the relevant marginal cost curve for decision making is cc'. Any output decided upon must be divided equally among the three plants since, in the absence of compensation from the others, none of the oligopolists will consent to shut down or to accept a smaller market share than the other two. Curve cc' is drawn on the assumption that every output is divided equally among the three plants.

If the industry's marginal revenue curve is given by R_2R_2' in Figure 3-8, it is clear that monopoly and oligopoly will produce the same result. At outputs greater than OX_3 the monopolist and oligopolists have the same marginal cost curve. Equating marginal cost and marginal revenue, they will both produce an output OX_4 and gain the same profit.

For outputs of less than OX_3, however, monopoly and oligopoly give different results. Should the industry's marginal revenue curve be R_1R_1', the oligopolists will produce OX_2, whereas the multiplant monopolist, faced with the marginal revenue curve R_1R_1', will reduce his variable costs by closing one plant and then use two plants to produce an output OX_1. In short, when the industry's marginal revenue curve is R_1R_1', the monopolist produces a smaller output than would oligopoly. But he produces it in a technically more efficient manner, that is, at a lower unit cost, and so realizes a greater profit.

When the industry's marginal revenue curve is R_1R_1' in Figure 3-8, is monopoly "better" than oligopoly? If we invoke a naive welfare test, the answer is that monopoly may—or may not—be better. By our usage, a naive welfare test is one that involves using the area under the industry's demand curve as a measure of consumer benefit, and the total cost of output as a measure of the social costs incurred to produce it. Such a test is naive not in the sense of being a less trustworthy guide to social policy than more complicated measures of consumer welfare which require even greater amounts of unobtainable information. It is naive only in the sense that it ignores the so-called neighborhood effects of production, for example, the fact that any increase in the waste products of one industry may raise unit cost of production in other industries.

When a naive welfare test is used, whether monopoly is to be preferred to oligopoly depends upon the slopes that we assign to the curve of marginal revenue and the respective unit cost curves of the industry organized as a monopoly and as an oligopoly. It would be tedious to write down the conditions that must be satisfied in order for monopoly to be better than oligopoly, and we shall not do it. In any event, as many writers have pointed out, neither monopoly nor oligopoly is an optimum solution by the naive welfare test. Maximum consumer welfare could be obtained only by building plants and expanding output until long-run marginal cost becomes equal to price in the industry.

Now suppose that the demand for the industry's product regularly fluctuates between R_1R_1' and R_2R_2' in Figure 3-8. On this premise it is clear that the members of the industry will not be indifferent between organizing themselves as monopoly and as oligopoly. For if the industry is to maximize profit, output must fluctuate between OX_1 and OX_4; whereas, since none of the three oligopolists will close down so long as total revenue exceeds total variable costs, when the industry is organized as an oligopoly, output will only fluctuate between OX_2 and OX_4.

In effect, the power of monopoly to open and close plants in response to changing demand is a *bona fide* economy of scale. Indeed, one would expect that, in the absence of antitrust restrictions on mergers, oligopoly would rapidly give way to monopoly in any industry subject to wide seasonal or cyclical fluctuations in demand; and there is, in fact, considerable evidence that, before the merger provisions of the American antitrust laws were given teeth, mergers were used to secure greater flexibility in the planning of production in response to changes in demand.[5]

5 · THE EXCLUSION OF OLIGOPOLY FROM STATIC THEORY. Let us briefly sum up. Given the usual assumptions of static economic theory and the special assumption that new firms are barred from entering, a multiplant industry will be (or will rapidly become) a multiplant monopoly whatever its initial organization. Such a monopoly can take any number of legal forms; it may, for example, be constituted as a profit-maximizing oligopoly, a cartel, a holding company, or a large corporation. Of course the choice of legal form does not affect the determination of the industry's equilibrium price, output, or profit. Strictly speaking, economic theory knows nothing of legal form, only "firms." In the next chapter we shall find that, when entry is free into a multiplant industry, it also will be (or will rapidly become) a single multiplant firm or cartel. Such an enterprise will have the appearance of monopoly but does not deserve the name. For, to say the obvious, it will dare not charge the same high price as would a protected monopolist for fear of attracting new firms.

---

[5] See, for example, J. W. Jenks, "The Development of the Whiskey Trust," *Political Science Quarterly,* IV (1889), 297–319. Jenks (an indifferent theorist but an accurate observer) emphasizes that the trust's ability to open and close distilleries in response to variations in demand gave it an efficiency advantage over the loosely organized "pool" which preceded it.

What have we done to oligopoly? After all, since the pioneer researches into duopoly by Cournot, economists have often pondered the determination of price and output in industries where sellers are few; and, in the last three decades, many able economists have been engaged in the search for *the* theory of oligopoly. Yet our analysis implies that, on the assumptions of static economic theory (with or without the postulate of free entry), an industry in equilibrium will consist of one firm.

That oligopoly exists in the real world is a fact of economic life. But I believe that in trying to explain it we ought to keep two truths in mind. The first is that oligopoly, especially as it operates in the United States (which, for better or worse, has provided most of the illustrative material on oligopoly), is largely a product of the American antitrust laws. There is nothing natural about the stable coexistence of the Big Three, Big Four, and so on. A rapid consolidation and rationalization of such industries would follow the repeal of the American legal restrictions on mergers and cartels. The truth relevant to the study of oligopoly is that such oligopoly as would survive a return to a legal code of laissez-faire would owe its continued existence to the fact of uncertainty in the business world. If all firms in an industry were in complete agreement about what the future would bring, they would agree on a common course of action designed to maximize their joint profits. It is only because such consensus is not possible in the real world that some oligopoly would survive the repeal of the antitrust laws. The persistence of oligopoly in a legal environment of laissez-faire would merely signify that the members of an industry had individually concluded that the prospective gains associated with contractual freedom were greater than the payoff promised by a policy of joint maximization. In fine, oligopoly is a phenomenon of permanent "disequilibrium" which has no place in static theory.

CHAPTER 4 *Stable Equilibrium in Imperfect Competition*

1 · THE INSTABILITY OF TANGENCY SOLUTIONS. In Chapter 2 the argument was developed that, on the assumptions usually employed in economic theory, the treatment of imperfect competition in terms of the "tangency solution" is both ambiguous and erroneous. It is ambiguous in that, when entry into an industry is free, a great number of no-profit-no-loss equilibria are possible, each dictated by how the firms are presumed to react to one another's changes in price and output. We saw that the widely used premise that one firm "ignores" the possible reaction of rival producers can mean only that it assumes that they will not react at all—in which case the firm regards the unused portion of the industry demand curve as its own. (To assume that the firm is so deluded that it fails to perceive any connection between industry demand and its own production problem would be to contradict our assumption that all firms have perfect knowledge of the market.) The tangency solution is erroneous in that it implies that an equilibrium with technically inefficient production can be stable, whereas, in fact, when there are no antitrust type restrictions on freedom of contract—and no peasant-type folkways that impede income-maximization—a tangency solution can only be a temporary stop on the way to a stable equilibrium.[1]

In Chapter 2 we derived two different tangency solutions to show the existence of multiple equilibria. At that time, however, the instability of all tangency solutions was merely asserted. In this chapter we turn to three important items of unfinished business. We must (1) show why all tangency solutions are unstable, (2) prove that a stable equilibrium not involving tangency can exist in an imperfectly competitive market, and (3) assuming that a stable equilibrium can exist, show what it is.

It is no difficult task to demonstrate that, on the usual assumptions of economic theory, every tangency solution is unstable. We need only show that, for every organization of the industry implied by a tangency solution, there is another organization of the industry which (a) its member firms prefer because it is technically more efficient and hence more profitable and (b) allows the production of an output which will discourage the entry of new firms.

Note that we here define "equilibrium" in terms of the organization of the industry rather than in terms of price and output. This choice of words is deliberate. We shall presently find that, as a tangency solution gives way to stable equilibrium, there are concomitant changes in the industry's output,

---

[1] This chapter offers, I believe, the most detailed exposition of the argument that all tangency solutions are unstable that has yet appeared. But the main features of the argument have been sketched on at least two earlier occasions. I first developed the argument (very inelegantly) for competition made imperfect by transport costs in "Imperfect Competition No Bar to Efficient Production," *Journal of Political Economy*, LXVI (1958), 24–33; and the argument was used by Harold Demsetz to call into question the validity of Chamberlin's proposition that product differentiation must lead to excess capacity. "The Nature of Equilibrium in Monopolistic Competition," *Journal of Political Economy*, LXVII (1959), 21–30.

number of plants, and number of firms. The most striking impact of this evolution, however, will be upon the number of firms.[2]

If competition is truly imperfect, the organizational equilibrium implied by a tangency solution must be unstable. The necessity of this result can be most easily seen by supposing that all plants in an imperfectly competitive industry are, by a wave of the economist's wand, placed under unified central management. Such a management would, of course, secure its lowest possible unit cost by producing some multiple of the output that minimizes unit cost in a single plant. (We retain our convenient assumption that there is only one way to build a plant.)

In Chapter 3 we saw that, when all plants are identical and each plant produces an output that permits it to operate in the neighborhood of minimum unit cost, the unit cost curve of a firm with n plants $(n > 1)$ is obtained by summing the unit cost curves of its n plants. We write P for price, U_1 for unit cost in the one-plant firm, and U_n for unit cost in the n-plant firm. Then there must exist a range of output such that $P - U_n > 0$ and $P - U_1 < 0$. This result is illustrated by Figure 4-1.

In Figure 4-1, AA' is the curve of unit cost in the n-plant firm, and OM gives the output beyond which it pays to operate all n plants. BB' is the curve of unit cost for a one-plant firm so located that its minimum point coincides with the minimum

---

[2] The practice of conducting economic analysis in terms of "firms" and "plants" is the legacy of a technologically simpler age. However, the practice does no harm provided that we realize that these terms no longer have quite the same meanings in economics that they had sixty years ago in the business world. To an economist a firm is an autonomous enterprise that combines "factors" in order to produce a "product"; and a plant is any piece of equipment which the firm has acquired by incurring a fixed cost. That is, a plant can be conceived of as a factory, shop, building, truck, or machine—or even a vice-president with an airtight contract that guarantees him some minimum annual income for ten years.

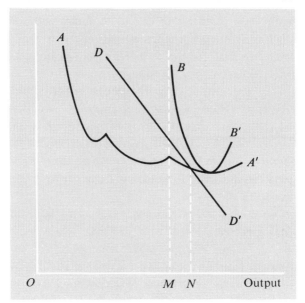

Figure 4-1

point of AA'. Demand for the industry's product is given by
DD'. We see that, when the n-plant firm produces an output
between OM and ON, then $P - U_n > 0$, since over this range
of output DD' lies above AA'. Yet over the same range of output DD' lies below BB'; hence $P - U_1 < 0$. Thus an n-plant
firm is always in a position to enforce a price that allows it a
profit but is low enough to discourage a prospective newcomer
from acquiring a plant and entering the industry.

2 · THE MEANING OF "FREE ENTRY." Let us accept
that every tangency solution implies an organization of an
imperfectly competitive industry that is unstable. Can we now
proceed to show that a stable equilibrium exists and describe its
properties? Let us approach this task with the hunch that there,

as in most problems of economic analysis, the answer that we shall derive depends upon the assumptions that we make. Actually, to describe the properties of a stable equilibrium in an imperfectly competitive industry we need only to clarify one of the assumptions already introduced, namely, the assumption of free entry. When we say that entry into an industry is "free," we shall mean that the entry of new firms is an instantaneous possibility. That is, whenever a prospective newcomer to the industry sees that he can enter the industry and at least break even (in the sense of having price equal to or greater than unit cost), he will do so.

No doubt, the premise that free entry is instantaneous entry does great violence to reality. Nevertheless, it is an immensely useful, indeed indispensable, assumption in economic theory. If we decline to use it, we are forced to adopt one of two alternatives. We may accept that, although entry is not instantaneous, entry nevertheless proceeds at a known rate. This assumption would compel us to abandon geometry for algebra without conferring any compensating benefits in new insights. The entry of new firms would "ultimately" eliminate (most) monopoly profit, but the established firm would have to revise its price-output policy whenever a new firm entered.

As a second possibility, we could assume that entry is impeded in that high profits will probably draw new firms into the industry, but nobody knows in advance at what rate or in what numbers. The case of impeded entry is not unimportant, and we consider it in some detail in Chapter 6; but, of course, impeded entry is incompatible with the assumptions of static economic theory since it is rooted in the uncertainty of the real world. Given the limited objective of our present analysis, the simplest thing to do is to equate free entry with instantaneous entry and, so to speak, give every investor an all-purpose

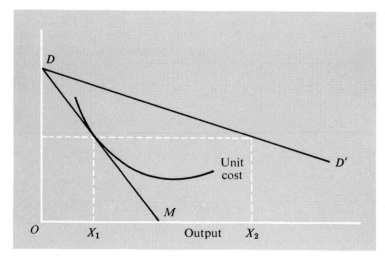

Figure 4-2

Meccano set in his basement that can be transformed into any sort of plant whenever a monopoly profit is discerned.[3]

3 · THE TRANSFORMATION OF TANGENCY SOLUTION A. On the premise that free entry is instantaneous entry, we can easily trace the steps by which a tangency solution evolves (or decays) into a stable equilibrium. Figure 4-2

[3] W. F. Stolper once argued that there cannot be stable equilibrium in monopolistic or imperfect competition except on assumptions "so restrictive as to make the concept virtually meaningless." I believe, however, that Stopler erred in two respects. First, he ascribed the impossibility of equilibrium to product differences, whereas the real culprit is the fact that entry is not an instantaneous possibility. If such entry is possible, an equilibrium is conceivable for a rationalized industry that produces differentiated products. Second, I think that economists must deny that because no real-world industry ever achieves equilibrium is no reason for concluding that the concept of equilibrium

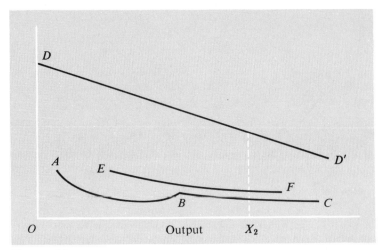

Figure 4-3

depicts the case of tangency solution A—the case where every producer knows that his change in output (or price) will immediately be matched by all rivals. Let the industry initially consist of four firms. Thus in Figure 4-2 the demand curve for the industry's product is given by DD', whereas the demand curve for the single firm is given by DM, which has four times the slope of DD'.

In Figure 4-2 each firm produces an output OX_1; and the four firms together produce an output OX_2. Clearly there has been overinvestment in the industry in the sense that production is technically inefficient: the cost of producing OX_2 would now be less if, in the beginning, its production had been entrusted to a single producer who would have built less than four plants.

In Figure 4-3 the "scallop" curve ABC shows what a portion

is not useful for illuminating some features of "reality." See W. F. Stolper, "The Possibility of Equilibrium under Monopolistic Competition," *Quarterly Journal of Economics,* LIV (1940), 519–26.

of the curve average variable cost would be for a cartel or single firm that owned all four plants. Curve EF is a portion of the curve obtained by summing up the curve of average variable cost of the four plants on the assumption that all are used. At output OX_2, curve EF lies above curve $ABC;$ hence it is more efficient to produce output OX_2 in two plants than in four plants. (Recall that if n be the number of kinks in the curve of average variable cost to the left of a given point, the number of plants which it pays to operate at that output is equal to $n + 1$.)

Suppose now that our four independent firms, each operating one plant, are merged, gathered into a profit-maximizing cartel, or otherwise placed under unified central management. We have seen that such a "monopolist" could produce a number of outputs more cheaply than our independents; and that there is a subset of this number for which price is greater than unit cost for the monopolist but less than unit cost for any prospective newcomer. The problem is to find the output which minimizes the amount of profit that the monopolist must sacrifice in order to discourage the entry of a rival. There is no reason why this output should be the same as the output of a tangency solution. Figure 4-4 illustrates one of the many possible ways of reckoning the output of stable equilibrium in imperfect competition: (a) Draw line SS' parallel to DD' (the industry demand curve) and tangent to the unit cost curve of the single plant; (b) from the intercept of SS' and the y-axis draw line SM parallel to the x-axis; (c) from point M draw line MX_4 normal to the x-axis.

Now we see that the output of our imperfectly competitive industry is, in stable equilibrium, slightly greater than the distance OX_3, and that the price corresponding to this equilibrium output will be slightly less than the distance OS. These conclusions follow since the demand curve for the potential entrant is the "unused" portion of the demand curve DD' of the "monopolist." When the latter produces in excess of OX_3 there is no output at which the potential entrant can cover unit cost. The defeat of the potential entrant is illustrated by Figure 4-5. When the monopolist produces an output slightly in excess of OX_3 in Figure 4-4, the demand curve for the potential entrant is dd' in Figure 4-5. It is everywhere below unit cost.

To sum up: In our example, as tangency solution A gives way to stable equilibrium via mergers or cartels, (a) average variable cost and, hence, unit cost fall; (b) the number of plants operated falls from four to two; (c) the industry that initially consisted of four firms is transformed into something that looks like a monopoly but really is not; and (d) output increases from OX_2 to OX_3 (Figures 4-3 and 4-4). Since every plant represents a fixed cost, any example will suffice to illustrate the lowering of variable and unit cost, the shutdown of plants, and the transition to apparent monopoly as the industry

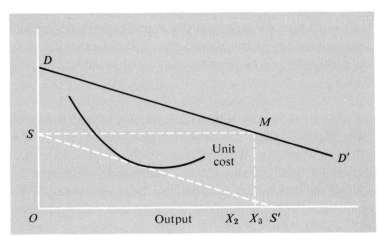

Figure 4-4

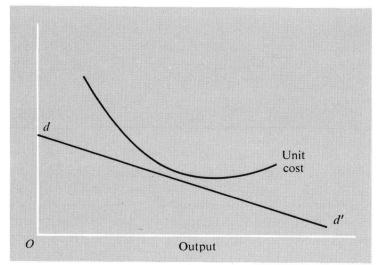

Figure 4-5

moves from tangency solution A to stable equilibrium. There is, however, no necessity that the process should produce an increase in industry output, as in our example. Depending upon the properties of thc industry demand curve and the unit cost curve of the plant, the transition will be accompanied by an increase, a decrease, or no change at all in output.

4 · THE TRANSFORMATION OF TANGENCY SOLU- TION B. Only a brief discussion of the transformation of tangency solution B into stable equilibrium is needed since the same process of rationalization via mergers and cartels described above is involved. Recall that tangency solution B requires the peculiar world of Cournot in which each producer (a) assumes that the unused portion of the industry demand curve is the same as his own over the relevant price range; (b)

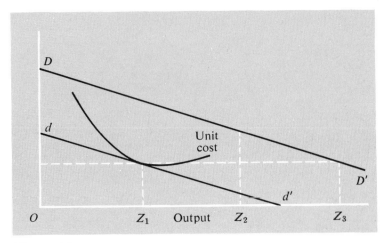

Figure 4-6

believes that he can change his own output without causing
rival firms to change their outputs; (c) is mistaken in this
belief; and (d) does not learn from experience that he is
mistaken.

In Figure 4-6 line DD' gives a segment of the aggregate
demand curve for an industry that consists of three firms.
Line dd' gives the demand curve that each of the three firms
erroneously believes that it faces. Each firm produces OZ_1, and
the three firms together produce an output OZ_3. If distance
Z_2Z_3 be equal to distance OZ_1, a monopolist who takes over
the industry will reduce variable cost by closing one of the
three plants and using the other two to produce an output
slightly greater than OZ_2. We note that tangency solution B differs from tangency solution A in that, in tangency solution B,
output *always* falls as stable equilibrium is approached. Here
we can be quite precise. If X^* denotes the industry output in
tangency solution B, and x^* the output of a single plant in

tangency solution B, the industry's output after the rationalization that secures stable equilibrium will be slightly in excess of X^*-x^*. (We return to this point in the appendix to this chapter.)

5 · THE DIVISION OF JOINT PROFITS. In recent years the problem of dividing the gains resulting from the formation of a merger or cartel has received no little attention.[4] Strictly speaking, the problem is "indeterminate" in that any one of the parties to the negotiations can sabotage the goal of maximum profit by refusing to cooperate; consequently his share may depend upon bargaining power, bargaining skill, or his "reasonableness." (The usual assumption is that the reasonable man will have to accept lower shares to gain the cooperation of his unreasonable brother.)

That the formation of mergers and cartels has often been associated with long and difficult negotiations is true enough. But the difficulties have mostly arisen because the different parties have reached different conclusions about the future profitability of the industry. Thus, when the United States Steel Corporation was organized in 1901, a finance problem arose because the pessimistic Andrew Carnegie demanded and received payment in cash and bonds (rather than stocks) as his price for parting with his interest in the Carnegie steel works.

Nevertheless, as a practical matter, it is virtually impossible that joint profit maximization will not be established when all

[4] See, for example, J. F. Nash, Jr., "The Bargaining Problem," *Econometrica*, XVIII (1950), 155–62; J. C. Harsanyi, "Approaches to the Bargaining Problem Before and After the Theory of Games," *Econometrica*, XXIV (1956), 144–57, and "A Simplified Bargaining Model for the *n*-Person Cooperative Game," *International Economic Review*, IV (1963), 194–220.

producers have come to believe that it will raise their aggregate income. The "obvious" method is simply to distribute joint profits in proportion to the investment contribution of each party. Should there be differences of opinion respecting the proper valuation of investment contributions, the issues can be settled in any number of ways, most notably by majority vote, tossing a coin, or resort to arbitration. The process by which an exact division of joint profits is secured is a subject of infinite interest to students of bargaining, but it need not detain us. Once all parties have decided that a shift to joint profit maximization can make everybody better off, we can be confident that it will come to pass sooner or later. Any other outcome would contradict the assumption that the industry is in the hands of economically rational managers.

The preceding discussion of how tangency solutions A and B give way to a stable and technically efficient equilibrium implicitly assumes that the contract costs needed to arrange the transition are zero. Contract costs include, *inter alia,* the legal and accounting charges generated by a merger or cartel and the managerial time that must be devoted to the requisite negotiations. When contract costs are not zero, and one begins with tangency solution A or B, it is possible that complete technical efficiency will never be achieved. This is only to say that, in such a situation, producers may find it advisable to continue to live indefinitely with some of the investment mistakes of the past (just as the railroad managements of most countries have resigned themselves to the standard track gauge of four feet, eight-and-one-half inches—too narrow for optimum use of modern technology—bequeathed to them by nineteenth-century engineers). In a static model, however, it is reasonable to assume that contract costs are zero since all producers have the same goals and act upon the basis of the same information.

6 · A BACKWARD GLANCE. I hope that the foregoing description of how stable equilibrium is achieved under conditions of imperfect competition has at least novelty of presentation. But of course the main ingredients from which it was constructed have been in the public domain of economic ideas for a great many years. Indeed, the thesis that, as long as it enjoys no legal protection against the entry of other producers, an established firm may have "the possibility of the form of monopoly without the power of it" was long ago beautifully expressed by J. B. Clark.[5]

A business . . . may have the form of monopoly, but not its genuine power. It may consolidate into one great corporation all the producers of an article who send their goods into a general market, and if no rivals of this corporation then appear, the public is forced to buy from it whatever it needs of the particular kind of goods which it makes . . . Yet the price may conceivably be a normal

---

[5] While J. B. Clark never succeeded in gaining for the idea of potential competition the attention that he thought it deserved, it never sank very far from view. Thus, in *Industry and Trade* (3rd ed., London, 1920), p. 397, Marshall writes: "It will in fact presently be seen that, though monopoly and free competition are ideally wide apart, yet in practice they shade into one another by imperceptible degrees: that there is an element of monopoly in nearly all competitive business: and that nearly all the monopolies, that are of any practical importance in the present age, hold much of their power by an uncertain tenure; so that they would lose it ere long, if they ignored the possibilities of competition, direct and indirect." For other reasonably explicit recognitions of the economic effects of potential competition see J. M. Clark, *Studies in the Economics of Overhead Costs* (Chicago, 1923), pp. 444–48; J. B. Bain, "A Note on Pricing in Monopoly and Oligopoly," *American Economic Review,* XXXIX (1949), 448–64; W. A. Leeman, "The Limitations of Local Price-Cutting as a Barrier to Entry," *Journal of Political Economy,* LXIV (1956), 329–40; Bjarke Fog, "Stayout Pricing," *Metroeconomica,* IX (1957), 42–51; and Paola Sylos-Labini, *Oligopoly and Technical Progress* (Cambridge, 1962), pp. 40–50.

one. It may stand not much above the cost of production to the monopoly itself. If it does so, it is because a higher price would invite competition. The great company prefers to sell all the goods that are required at a moderate price than to invite rivals into its territory. This is monopoly in form but not in fact, for it is shorn of its injurious power; and the thing that holds it firmly in check is *potential competition.* The fact that a rival *can* appear and *will* appear if the price goes above the reasonable level at which it stands, induces the corporation to produce goods enough to keep the price at that level. Under such a nearly ideal condition the public would get the full benefit of the economy which very large production gives, notwithstanding that no actual competition would go on.[6]

7 · SOME IMPLICATIONS OF THE ANALYSIS. Should the difference between total cost and total revenue that appears when tangency solutions A and B give way to stable equilibrium be termed "monopoly profit" or simply a "rent inherent in the existence of fixed costs in the plant"? While the label favored is mostly a matter of terminological taste, my own preference is for calling it a rent. This term has not the sinister overtones of monopoly profit and conveys that the residual described is neither accidental nor temporary. Regardless of what the difference between total cost and total revenue is called, the analysis offered above has a number of distinctly radical implications for the way in which economists view the process of competition.

First, it shows that, on the assumptions usually employed in static economic theory, "monopoly" rather than the presence of more than one firm is the natural condition of the "industry." Indeed, as we noted in Chapter 3, in static economic theory

[6] *Essentials of Economic Theory* (New York, 1907), pp. 380–81.

there is no place for oligopoly save as a form of disequilibrium.[7]

Second, it shows that, on such assumptions, the only significant difference between perfect competition and imperfect competition lies in the number of plants which an industry can support. When the object is to demonstrate how equilibrium price and output are achieved, the premise that the industry consists of a great number of firms is, from a pedagogical viewpoint, excess baggage. Worse, it is costly excess baggage. It can cause one to ignore the need for centralized control of plant operations if production is to be technically efficient, and to lose sight of the role that mergers, cartels, and subcontracting play in the competitive process.

Third, our analysis of how tangency solutions give way to stable equilibrium provides a warning against the mechanical application of naive criteria of economic welfare to policy problems of economic organization. There may, of course, be persuasive arguments for preventing mergers among, for example, large cement firms in the United States, as the Federal Trade Commission is so assiduously doing. Yet to the extent that entry into the cement industry is "free," such restrictions, at best, cause the industry's output to be produced at a higher unit cost and, at worst, cause output to be reduced below the level that a laissez-faire policy would bring about.

In this connection we might emphasize that the results ob-

---

[7] We find an earlier perception of this truth in Heinrich von Stackelberg's treatment of duopoly "Duopoly is an unstable market form not only in the sense that price is apt to be indeterminate, but much more because it is unlikely to remain as a market form for any length of time. The inherent contradictions in the duopolistic situation press for a solution through the adoption of another market form— monopoly." *The Theory of the Market Economy,* translated from the German by A. T. Peacock (New York, 1952), p. 203.

tained in this chapter do not depend upon the assumption that there is an approximation to a constant unit cost of output, that is, that output can be expanded without raising unit cost by building additional plants. Sometimes it is said that the existence of increasing unit cost in the firm is sufficient to ensure the existence of competition in the sense that an industry then consists of more than one seller. This is not quite right. Our conclusion is that unified central management of the whole industry is the normal result of laissez-faire when no diseconomies of management characterize the enterprise. This conclusion holds even if the expansion of output raises the prices of its factor inputs and so makes it an "increasing cost industry." In order to prevent the emergence of unified central management, it is necessary that n plants operated by more than on firm can produce a given output more cheaply than the same n plants under unified central management.

Finally, our analysis of imperfect competition that runs in terms of stay-out pricing can be employed to throw light on yet another venerable and important puzzle in applied economics. American economists have been intrigued by the fact that, often in many industries of high ownership concentration, the growth of demand is not accompanied by the entry of new firms. That is, once a pattern of apparent monopoly or oligopoly has been established, it tends to persist even though the growth of demand might seem to provide opportunities for profit that would attract newcomers. (In the American economy, examples of tenacious oligopolies in expanding industries can be found in cigarettes, steel, meat packing, soap and detergents, and, of course, automobiles.)

Yet, is there really a conundrum here? Suppose that by a simple change in our assumptions we convert our stable equilibrium for an imperfectly competitive industry into a growth model. This we do by positing that henceforth demand for the industry's product will grow exponentially at some given rate. We leave technology unchanged, and continue to assume that there are neither economies nor diseconomies of plant management. Now it is clear that both investment and output in the industry must expand in response to the growth of demand. The only question is whether the provision of additional plant and output will be made by the established firm (which may be profit-sharing cartel) or by new firms.

A moment's reflection will show that the established firm will maximize profit by taking the initiative itself and providing all of the additional investment and output. For if new firms enter the industry, the result will be an organizational disequilibrium characterized by technical inefficiency; and, to escape the wastes of a tangency solution, a new program of rationalization will have to be worked out involving a profit-sharing arrangement between the established firm and the newcomers. This arrangement, of course, will require payment of compensation to owners of plants to be shut and hence will be privately and socially wasteful. More important for our immediate analysis, the need to compensate investors who have supplied the industry with excess capacity will reduce the rate of profit of the old, established firm. This unfortunate result can easily be avoided by the established firm. It need only adopt the simple expedient of providing itself the additional output needed to meet the rise in demand.

The interesting question is not why new firms do not enter highly concentrated industries in great numbers as demand grows, but rather why even a few make the hazardous effort. A plausible answer is that the entry of new firms occurs when the future of the industry is generally thought to be bright but highly uncertain—a situation which, happily, is fairly common in the real world.

If the established firm really believes that it can predict the future for its product and, equally important, if most investors also believe that it has this power, then it will "normally" forestall the entry of new firms by increasing its own investment and output. Only when there are widespread differences of opinion about the future (as, for example, when the nature of the product is changing rapidly) will new firms get their chance. But, of course, as the passing of time makes the unknown known, all the incentives to secure the economies of rationalization through mergers and cartels will reassert themselves. Thus it is not really surprising that, in many industries in the years 1910–1950, the growth of demand under conditions of much uncertainty saw the formation of new firms which, however, soon failed, turned to the production of other products, or merged with older firms. Statistically, the result appeared to be a rather stable pattern of oligopoly in this period.[8]

The preceding observations are limited to the years 1910–1950 because antitrust policy, as interpreted by the federal courts, then favored the perpetuation of oligopoly; that is, this policy permitted big firms to acquire small rivals but not big rivals. Before 1910 the virtual absence of antitrust restrictions on mergers was rapidly replacing oligopoly with the so-called dominant firm pattern in the heavy industry sector of the economy; whereas, because of the tightening noose of antitrust, since 1950 big firms (say the 500 largest non-financial corporations) have had great difficulty in acquiring even small rivals.

[8] M. A. Adelman, "The Measurement of Industrial Concentration," *Review of Economics and Statistics,* XXXIII (1951), 269–96; G. W. Nutter, *The Extent of Enterprise Monopoly in the United States: 1899–1939* (Chicago, 1951); and H. A. Einhorn, "Competition in American Industry, 1939–58," *Journal of Political Economy,* LXXIV (1966), 506–11.

In recent years the outstanding feature of oligopoly has continued to be its stability. And, notwithstanding the eloquent and insistent affirmations of J. K. Galbraith to the contrary, the modest movement that has occurred since 1950 has been in the direction of J. M. Clark's workable competition.

8 · PITFALLS IN THE INTERPRETATION OF EMPIRICAL COST DATA. In our discussion of how stable equilibrium comes to an imperfectly competitive industry, there remains one important item of unfinished business. Judgments about the efficiency (or lack of it) in an industry are necessarily based upon what we assume to be the curves of unit cost for the single plant and for the multiplant firm. Yet, even when neither economies nor diseconomies are to be had by bringing additional plants under unified central management, some serious errors can result if we fail to recall a simple truth. Unit cost means one thing to the builder of an economic model and something different to an accountant or econometrician who constructs cost functions from accounting data.

The crucial difference is that unit cost as defined in economic theory excludes all rent or profit elements, that is, payments not needed to secure the resources needed for production. To the accountant, however, unit cost includes all outlays which the owners of an enterprise have expended to produce a given output. Thus it can include elements which, from the economic theorist's standpoint, are profit or rent. In fact, as the control of property changes hands by sale or lease, the usual system of accounting converts the profit or rent realized by initial owners into the fixed costs of later owners or lessees.

More specifically, as the control of property changes hands, two bookkeeping phenomena can be observed. Unit cost as reck-

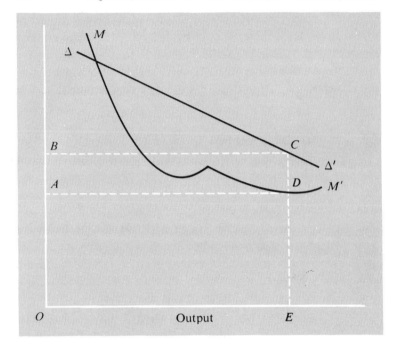

Figure 4-7

oned by accountants increases until it absorbs all profit (or rent), and the slope of the unit cost curve at any given output changes. The manner in which these results are brought about is illustrated in Figures 4-7 and 4-8. Here we have depicted a two-plant firm that has achieved stable equilibrium. It produces output *OE* in Figure 4-7 which sets price at *OB* and so discourages the entry of new firms. If the firm was the first to rationalize production in the industry, then its curve of unit cost may be taken as *MM'*, its demand curve as ΔΔ', and its monopoly profit (or rent) as the area *ABCD* in Figure 4-7.

Now let us suppose that the parties who first organized stable equilibrium lease their two plants to a syndicate of late comers. They will presumably charge a sum equal to the rent (or profit) that they could have realized by continuing to operate the two plants themselves, that is, they charge a sum equal to *ABCD* in Figure 4-7. To the accountants who set up the books of the new operators, this sum is an additional item of fixed cost and hence a part of unit cost. Thus in Figure 4-8 the unit cost curve of the enterprise under new management is *NN'*. The transfer does not, of course, affect equilibrium output because the new operators must continue to produce output *OE* in order to dissuade new firms from entering the industry. Rent (or profit)

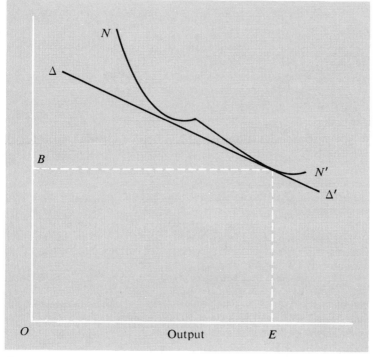

Figure 4-8

has not been obliterated, only absorbed into a higher curve of unit cost.[9]

We note also that the bookkeeping conversion of the original promoters of rent (or profit) into an element of fixed cost of the new operators can delude unwary observers into believing that the firm has excess capacity. As Figure 4-7 indicates, the firm in stable equilibrium produces an output OE that minimizes unit cost. Yet, as Figure 4-8 shows, after the rent $ABCD$ has been capitalized, the firm appears to be operating where unit cost is falling. This result is inevitable given that, before absorption of the charge $ABCD$, unit cost was at a minimum when output OE was produced. The additional new item of fixed cost ensures that unit cost appears to be minimized at an output that is now greater than OE.

One sobering reflection must be that the very great number of empirical studies that have sought to plot the unit cost curve of the firm have virtually no significance for economists.[10] They are all based upon accounting data and hence must be presumed to contain elements of rent and, to this extent, to falsify both the location and the shape of the unit cost curve. Empirical studies invariably conclude that most firms most of

[9] While the above truth may be simple, it is not obvious since it is ignored in most textbooks and treatises and is occasionally discovered in a professional journal. Martin Bronfenbrenner was, I believe, the first writer to offer a detailed demonstration of how cost curves in imperfect competition are affected by the capitalization of profit (or rent). See his "Imperfect Competition on a Long-Run Basis," *Journal of Business,* XXIII (1950), 81–93.

[10] For representative studies, see W. J. Eiteman and G. E. Guthrie, "The Shape of the Average Cost Curve," *American Economic Review,* XLII (1952), 832–38; and Joel Dean, *Statistical Determination of Costs with Special Reference to Marginal Costs* (Chicago, 1936). For surveys of empirical work on cost functions, see P. J. D. Wiles, *Price, Cost and Output* (Oxford, 1956), pp. 227–51; and John Johnston, *Statistical Cost Analysis* (New York, 1960), pp. 44ff.

the time operate where unit cost is falling. This result is usually interpreted to mean that the firms surveyed possess "excess capacity." A more plausible inference is simply that the capital market does an extremely efficient job of capitalizing rent (or profit) in the firms surveyed. Additional evidence must be produced before we can accept a finding that excess capacity really does exist.

Appendix · A NOTE ON STATIC EQUILIBRIUM

In this chapter we rather laboriously derived the equilibrium conditions for a multiplant industry under conditions of imperfect competition and complete information. Both caution and some repetition seemed to be advisable in view of the widely held but erroneous notion that an equilibrium achieved under these conditions has to be technically inefficient. Once, however, we have accustomed ourselves to thinking in terms of stay-out pricing and joint maximization of profits, we can travel much faster. Indeed, the task of describing equilibrium under conditions of imperfect competition and complete information then reduces to a simple exercise in calculus.

Equilibrium Output

Let

(a) $P = D(X)$ constrained by $D'(X) < 0$ and $D''(X) \leqq 0$ give demand for the industry's product (P denoting price and X output);

(b) $c = \lambda x^{-1} + \phi(x)$ constrained by $\lambda > 1$, $\phi(x) > 0$, $\phi'(x\dagger) = 0$, $\phi''(x\dagger) > 0$ give unit cost in the single plant;

(c) $x^0 = x$ when $dc/dx = 0$;

(d) $\eta = $ a very small quantity of X or x.

Our object is to find equilibrium output for the industry X_e, equilibrium output for the plant x_e, equilibrium number of plants N_e, and equilibrium profit π_e. We proceed as follows: Let X^* and x^* be the values for X and x that satisfy

$$D(X) - \lambda x^{-1} - \phi(x) = 0$$
$$D'(X) + \lambda x^{-2} - \phi'(x) = 0 \tag{1}$$

In economic terms X^* gives Cournot equilibrium for the industry and x^*, Cournot equilibrium for the single plant. By definition, stable or long-run equilibrium for the industry, X_e, is given by

$$X_e = X^* - (x^* - \eta) \tag{2}$$

Recall that the incremental η is needed in order to ensure that the industry's profit is low enough to discourage the entry of a new firm. If the incremental η is omitted in equation (2), then the industry would produce $X^* - x^*$, and a single new firm could enter the industry and exactly break even.

Proceeding, we write

$$\frac{X_e}{x^o} = Q + \frac{R_1}{x^o} \tag{3}$$

where Q is an integer and $R_1/x^o < 1$.

We have either

$$N_e = Q \tag{4}$$

or

$$N_e = Q + 1 \tag{5}$$

When $R_1 = 0$, then $N_e = Q$ and $x_e = x^o$. When $R_1 \neq 0$, we must compare

$$c(R_1) = \left[\lambda \left(x^o + \frac{R_1}{Q} \right)^{-1} + \phi \left(x^o + \frac{R_1}{Q} \right) \right] \tag{6}$$

and

$$c(R_2) = \left[\lambda \left(x^o - \frac{R_2}{Q+1} \right)^{-1} + \phi \left(x^o - \frac{R_2}{Q+1} \right) \right] \tag{7}$$

where R_2 is obtained from

$$\frac{X_e}{Q+1} = x^o - R_2 \tag{8}$$

When $c(R_1) < c(R_2)$, $N_e = Q$ and $x_e = x^o + (R_1/Q)$. Conversely, when $c(R_1) > c(R_2)$, $N_e = Q + 1$ and $x_e = x^o - [R_2/(Q+1)]$.

In economic terms, when $x_e = x^o + (R_1/Q)$, each plant operates where unit cost is rising; when $x_e = x^o - [R_2/(Q+1)]$, each plant operates where unit cost is falling; and, when $x_e = x^o$, each plant operates where unit cost takes its minimum value.

Equilibrium Profit

Should the industry begin production as a rationalized multiplant enterprise, equilibrium profit will, of course, be given by

$$\pi_e = [D(X_e) - \{(\lambda x_e^{-1} + \phi(x_e))\}]X_e \tag{9}$$

Should, however, equilibrium be approached from a competitive starting point, rationalization may require the closing of some plants and the assumption of their fixed costs by the rationalized enterprise. We let N_k denote the number of plants in the industry before rationalization. Then, when the closed plants must be written off as a total loss,

$$\pi_e = [D(X_e) - \{\lambda x_e^{-1} + \phi(x_e)\}]X_e - \lambda(N_k - N_e) \tag{10}$$

Should it be possible to return the closed plants $(N_k - N_e)$ to production as some of the operating plants wear out, then, in equation (10), one would substitute $\alpha\lambda(0 < \alpha < 1)$ for λ, with α being a function of the average length of time that $(N_k - N_e)$ plants remained closed.

CHAPTER 5 *"Monopolistic" Competition as a Mathematical Complication*

1 · PRODUCT VARIETY AS AN ALLEGED SOURCE OF WASTE. The analysis of Chapter 4 established an important theorem and a corollary of nearly equal importance. When entry into an industry is free, all firms produce the same product, and Man or Nature has placed some restriction on freedom of contract, then, in the static case, we get an equilibrium with an output per plant of less than optimal amount. As we saw in Chapter 4, this is the "correct" formulation of the excess capacity theorem. That part of the technical inefficiency of this equilibrium which is traceable to an unkind Providence can only be endured. That part of inefficiency which is traceable to man-made restrictions on contractual freedom can, of course, be eliminated by removing them and allowing the search for profit to bring about rationalization of the industry's production.

The digression on product variety of this chapter is necessary mainly because of the historical accident that Edward Chamberlin first developed the tangency solution on the premise that, in monopolistic competition, rival firms produce a class of differentiated products—and because he so vehemently and persuasively insisted that it was product differentiation which distinguished "monopolistic" competition from "imperfect" competition. In his words, "The general conclusion must be that with a differentiated product the 'number of producers' ceases to have the definite meaning which it has in relation to any particular (standardized) product, and that broad generalization as to the effect of numbers upon the elasticities of the demand curves for individual producers is no longer possible." [1] Or, again, " 'Monopolistic competition' is a challenge to the traditional viewpoint of economics that competition and monopoly are alternatives and that individual prices are to be explained in terms of either the one or the other." [2]

The main question that we must resolve in this chapter is simply: When entry is free and no antitrust rules restrict the range of contractual freedom, does the fact that firms in an "industry" produce a set of differentiated products condemn it to technically inefficient production? If the answer is no (which it will be), then the claim that monopolistic competition is a phenomenon of the real world that requires for its study a special set of tools must be respectfully but emphatically denied. [3]

---

[1] *The Theory of Monopolistic Competition* (Cambridge, 5th ed., 1947), p. 198. See also *Towards a More General Theory of Value* (New York, 1957), pp. 43–69.

[2] *Monopolistic Competition*, p. 204.

[3] If the truths first described in articles in professional journals could readily find their way into standard textbooks and treatises, this chapter would be largely unnecessary. On two occasions Harold Demsetz has demonstrated that the equilibrium of the firm producing a differentiated product in Chamberlin's analysis is inherently unstable precisely because it contains excess capacity and hence can be rationalized. "The Nature of Equilibrium in Monopolistic Competition," *Journal of Political Economy*, LXVII (1959), 21–30, and "The Welfare and Empirical

2 · A MINOR PROBLEM OF METHODOLOGY. We might note that the importance attached by Chamberlin to product differentiation inspired the debate among economists over the respective merits of "an industry consisting of firms which produce a homogeneous product" and "a group of firms which produce different varieties of the same basic product" as tools for analyzing price making in the real world. Young readers may well have difficulty in deciding what the controversy was all about. Indeed, it can now be seen to make sense only on the premise that price making should be analyzed with the aid of two-dimensional geometry. If this restriction is accepted, the heuristic advantage in assuming away product variety in order to obtain a homogeneous product is impressive. For only by eliminating product differences can the cost and revenue functions of one firm be compared directly with those of all others (since, in each firm, total cost and total revenue are solely a function of total "output").

Simple geometry may be incapable of handling the concept of "an industry which produces a differentiated product." Simple algebra and calculus contain no such limitation. It is necessary to assume only that there exists a "basic product" which can be differentiated by expending additional resources on sales effort in the form of advertising, packaging, special

Implications of Monopolistic Competition," *Economic Journal,* LXXIV (1964), 623–41. See also his note, "Do Competition and Monopoly Differ?" *Journal of Political Economy,* LXXVI (1968), pp. 146–48.

My only criticism of Demsetz is that his work seems to imply that, in monopolistic competition, the "true" equilibrium with technically efficient production will see all profit eliminated, whereas, for the reasons indicated in Chapter 4, the presence of a fixed cost in the plant ensures only that "some" or "most" profit will be eliminated by rationalization and stay-out pricing.

accessories, sales on credit, warranties, advice to buyers, etc.[4] From the engineer's standpoint, any quantity of a basic product can always be differentiated. From the economist's standpoint, expenditures to differentiate will not be made unless they increase the total revenue that can be obtained from the sale of a given quantity of the basic product. Hence, virtually by definition, a homogeneous product is one whose average revenue per unit of basic product cannot be increased by such outlays.

The substitution of algebra and calculus for geometry in the teaching of economics is sometimes hard on beginning students. Since it creates only a minor scientific complication, however, there can be no serious objection to defining an industry as the set of all firms which produce different varieties of a basic product. But is this definition of an industry useful? When our purpose to study such phenomena as advertising, spatial competition, and product quality as an economic vari-

---

[4] My personal conclusion, based upon unhappy experience with alternatives, is that the analysis of product differentiation can be greatly simplified and clarified if it is viewed as the use of additional resources to increase the value of a basic product which has its own production function and demand curve. With this approach, "output" has only one meaning—it denotes output of the basic product; and one is preserved from the pitfall of attaching importance to comparisons of physical quantities of more differentiated and less differentiated forms of the basic product. Far too many textbooks contain the (virtually) meaningless statement that "the effect of monopolistic competition through product differentiation is to reduce output." The proper question is, of course, output of what? On the general methodology of product differences see Robert Triffin, *Monopolistic Competition and General Equilibrium Theory* (Cambridge, 1941), pp. 85–86; Hans Brems, *Some Problems of Monopolistic Competition* (Copenhagen, 1950), pp. 1–25; and Fritz Machlup, *The Economics of Sellers' Competition: Model Analysis of Sellers' Conduct* (Baltimore, 1952), pp. 164–77.

able, use of the definition is unavoidable. However, when our object is to understand how equilibrium is achieved through the use of stay-out pricing and rationalization of production, the need for the concept of an industry that produces a differentiated product is not self-evident. We shall conclude that the concept is excess baggage in this undertaking.

3 · EQUILIBRIUM WITH BENIGN PRODUCT DIFFERENCES. Let us begin by dividing all product differences into those which are benign and those which are *mala in se*. One may believe that the economy produces too many different models and brands of waffle iron without objecting in principle to "some" differentiation of the product. Differences of this sort are benign in that the only thing to be said against them is that they may cost "too much." In contrast, one may believe that any effort on anybody's part to suggest that a particular brand of aspirin is better than other brands is pernicious. Product differences of this sort are *mala in se* in that they would be objectionable even if no economic resources were used to create them.[5] We start with the case where all product differences are benign and so take consumers' tastes (including the idiocratic craving for variety) as data in a problem of cost minimization subject to constraint.

[5] Product differences which are *mala in se* include those based upon what some economists call (and condemn as) "exhortative" advertising. Non-exhortative advertising is, by implication, that which is confined to a decorous dissemination of accurate information about the seller's product. I prefer the awkward Latin borrowed from lawyers in the interest of greater generality, since not all forms of objectionable product variety can be traced to objectionable advertising. For a recent recitation of the case against Madison Avenue see C. D. Edwards, "Advertising and Competition: An Evaluation of Exhortative Programs," *Business Horizons,* XI (1968), 59–77.

For notation:

$$\sum_{1}^{n} x_i = X = \text{output of the "basic" product distributed among } n \text{ plants}$$

$$\sum_{1}^{m} s_i = S = \text{"effort" expended to differentiate } X \text{ that is distributed among } m \text{ marketing divisions}$$

u = minimum unit cost of producing x in the plant

v = minimum unit cost at which s can be secured in a marketing division

$R = MX - X^2$ = total revenue

$M = A + BS - S^2$, where A and B are constants

Hence,

$$R = AX + BXS - XS^2 - X^2$$

Let us be clear on the economic meaning of our assumptions. When $S = 0$, we have a linear demand curve for the basic product with M as the intercept of the curve and the price axis. Total revenue R can be increased by using resources to differentiate the output of the basic product X or any part of it. But, since $\partial^2 R/\partial S^2 < 0$, the creation of product variety is subject to diminishing returns. The assumption that the demand curve for the "product" can be shifted upward, albeit at a decreasing rate as sales effort is increased or quality improved, has characterized almost all discussions of monopolistic competition. In our exposition a linear demand curve for the basic product is employed for the sole purpose of simplifying the notation.

For convenience we also use S as a surrogate variable to represent all activities of the seller that serve to differentiate the basic product. We could, of course, write S_1 for visits by salesmen, S_2 for television advertising, S_3 for "free" visits by the seller's maintenance men, etc., and proceed. But we shall presently find that the mathematical problem of describing equilibrium in monopolistic competition becomes uncomfortably complicated when total revenue is treated as a function of only two independent variables.

We assume that in each plant the curve of unit cost of manufacturing the basic product is U-shaped, and also that in each marketing division the curve of unit cost of differentiating the basic product is U-shaped. If we take the final step and direct that, without incurring additional management costs, the firm can have more than one plant and more than one marketing division, then the total cost of manufacturing the basic product is approximately uX and the total cost of differentiating it is approximately vS.

We can now write

$$C = uX + vS = \text{total cost}$$

and

$$\tau = \frac{vS}{uX} = \text{``degree of product differentiation''}$$

By our assumptions, $\partial^2 R/\partial X^2 < 0$, $\partial^2 R/\partial S^2 < 0$ and there is a fixed cost in every plant and every marketing division. Hence stay-out pricing is possible for the centrally managed enterprise. That is, there is a profit Z ($Z > 0$) for such a firm that is low enough to discourage the entry of additional firms. Equilibrium in the industry is achieved when it minimizes

$$C = uX + vS \qquad (1)$$

subject to the constraint

$$AX + BSX - XS^2 - X^2 - uX - vS - Z = 0 \qquad (2)$$

(This operation is, of course, equivalent to maximizing R subject to the constraint that $R - C - Z = 0$.)

By the method of undetermined multipliers we obtain from equations (1) and (2)

$$u + \lambda(A + BS - S^2 - 2X - u) = 0$$
$$v + \lambda(BX - 2XS - v) = 0 \tag{3}$$

Thus

$$X = \frac{v(A + BS - S^2)}{(uB - 2uS + 2v)} \tag{4}$$

and

$$\tau = \frac{S(uB - 2uS + 2v)}{u(A + BS - S^2)} \tag{5}$$

Our first thought is to seek equilibrium values of X and S in terms of the coefficients in equation (2) by substituting the right side of equation (4) for X in equation (2) and then solving for S. Unhappily, this substitution yields an equation with a term that contains S^5, and a quintic equation has no general algebraic solution.[6] Thus the simplest formulation of the problem of optimizing subject to a profit constraint in monopolistic competition leads to an awkward mathematical complication. It is hardly surprising that product differentiation has caused economists so much trouble. But, of course, when numerical values are assigned to $A, B, Z, u,$ and v in equation (2), the equilibrium numerical values for S and X can be found or closely approximated by several methods.

If product differences are benign, presumably there is some amount of differentiation that is optional within the constraints of consumer tastes and the existing distribution of income. The problem of finding this optimum has not received much

[6] On the special class of equations of a degree higher than four that do have general algebraic solutions see H. W. Turnbull, *Theory of Equations* (London, 1939), pp. 114–16.

attention.[7] However, if we invoke naive welfare criteria—those which take consumer tastes and the existing distribution of income as given and ignore the neighborhood effects of production—the basic product must be optimally differentiated when total revenue R is maximized subject to $R - C = 0$.

In monopolistic competition the equilibrium values of S and X in equation (2) will necessarily be non-optimal (too low). Still, the greater the number of plants and marketing divisions that the rationalized enterprise operates in equilibrium, the closer will both the output of the basic product and the outlays made to differentiate it approximate the ideal. So, also, will τ, the "degree of product differentiation," approximate the ideal.

In this connection it is instructive to consider the behavior of $d\tau/dS$. We can write $\phi = uB + 2v$ and $\psi = uA$, substitute in equation (5), and obtain

$$\tau = \frac{\phi S - 2uS^2}{\psi + uBS - uS^2} \tag{5a}$$

Thus

$$\frac{d\tau}{dS} = \frac{\phi\psi - 4\psi uS - 2Bu^2S^2 + \phi uS^2}{(\psi + uBS - uS^2)^2} \tag{6}$$

[7] See, however, Robert Reichardt, "Competition through the Introduction of New Products," *Zeitschrift für Nationalökonomie,* XXII (1962), 41–84; and W. J. Baumol, "Calculation of Optimal Product and Retailer Characteristics: The Abstract Product Approach," *Journal of Political Economy,* LXXV (1967), 674–85. Both papers are concerned with the problem of tailoring the product that the individual firm faces in an oligopoly market. Earlier treatments of the optimizing problem without the complications of oligopoly are Robert Dorfman and P. O. Steiner, "Optimal Advertising and Optimal Quality," *American Economic Review,* XLIV (1954), 826–36, and N. S. Buchanan, "Advertising Expenditures: A Suggested Treatment," *Journal of Political Economy,* L (1942), 537–57.

In equation (6) the denominator is always positive. The numerator is negative for values of the coefficients which are "plausible," that is, values which will yield an equilibrium profit for the multiplant firm that is positive but in the neighborhood of zero. Thus $d\tau/dS$ "usually" takes a negative value.[8] Therefore, if the equilibrium of monopolistic competition is replaced by a legally protected monopoly that can dispense with stay-out pricing, S will decrease and the degree of product differentiation will usually increase. Likewise, if such an equilibrium is replaced by a state enterprise that respects and indulges consumer tastes for variety, S will increase and degree of product differentiation will usually decrease. The state enterprise which is so motivated will presumably act to maximize R subject to $R - C = 0$.

Should all expenditures to differentiate the basic product be outlawed by an antitrust rule that seeks to promote a more perfect competition, τ goes to zero, and X, the output of the basic product, decreases. The last result is dictated by our demand constraint, $R = AX + BXS - XS^2 - X^2$, because, for all economically significant values of S, $\partial R/\partial X$ varies directly with S and $\partial^2 R/\partial X^2$ is independent of S.[9]

---

[8] We can be more precise. When the numerator in equation (6) is zero, $d\tau/dS = 0$. We can set this numerator equal to zero, solve it as a quadratic in S, and discard the negative root. Then $d\tau/dS < 0$ when

$$S > \frac{2\psi u - [4\psi^2 u^2 - (\phi u - 2Bu^2)\phi\psi]^{1/2}}{\phi u - 2Bu^2}$$

[9] Professor Samuelson once noted that, in the case of a protected monopolist, an increase in advertising expenditure might be associated with a fall in the output of the basic product. *Foundations of Economic Analysis* (Cambridge, 1947), pp. 41–42. For this result to occur, the advertising expenditure would have simultaneously to raise the demand curve for the basic product and lower the corresponding marginal revenue curve. This would happen if, for example, advertising converted a linear demand curve into a "higher" demand curve that had unitary elasticity at all points, so that the monopolist could then maxi-

We note in passing that unnecessary confusion is often injected into the treatment of monopolistic competition by a failure to distinguish between the *amount* of product differentiation, S, and the *degree* of product differentiation, τ. In most cases, government rules and regulations which affect product variety probably have opposite effects on S and τ.

4 · ANTITRUST RULES AND PRODUCT VARIETY. Suppose that an antitrust rule is imposed that limits the number of plants and/or marketing divisions that a single firm can operate. One result must, of course, be technical inefficiency in manufacturing and/or marketing. It is not true, however, that another result must be "excessive" product differentiation in the sense that τ is higher than it would be if the industry were entrusted to a state enterprise that maximizes R subject to $R - C = 0$. The impact of an antitrust rule on τ depends upon the shape of the cost functions in the single plant and in the single marketing division—and upon how the less-than-optimal size firms view their respective revenue functions. An antitrust rule could well lead to "too little product variety." Even if the rule yields a τ which is optimal, it may, because of the higher costs that result, yield values for S and X which are too low. The only indisputably correct deduction is tautological. An antitrust rule that impairs manufacturing and/or marketing efficiency will cause the set of differentiated products to be inefficiently manufactured and/or marketed.

mize profit by producing the smallest amount of basic output that was technically feasible. In our analysis, however, S is a surrogate variable standing for *all* efforts to differentiate the basic product. And I believe it not unreasonable to assume that the primary net impact of these efforts is on the location rather than on the shape of the average revenue curve.

To sum up. The charge so often made in the last forty years that monopolistic competition leads to "too much" product variety and "excess" plant capacity is, when applied to a static model, misleading in three important respects.

1. Given no restrictions on mergers or cartels, any technical inefficiency that momentarily exists will be eliminated by the rationalization process described in Chapter 4. As we have seen, the mathematical notation needed to illustrate this process in an industry that produces a set differentiated products is more cumbersome than that which will suffice to illustrate it in an industry that produces a basic product only. Nevertheless, the process is essentially the same in both industries.

2. When a restriction on contractual freedom condemns the industry to the technical inefficiency of a tangency solution, product variety need not increase. For the reasons set down above, such an impediment to rationalization can also operate either to decrease the amount of product variety or to leave it unchanged.

3. When a restriction on contractual freedom leads to an increase or decrease in product variety, this change is merely a consolation prize offered by the market to unfortunate consumers. The change in product variety resulting from the antitrust rule is, by itself, wholly benign since it reduces the welfare impact of the rule. That is, the change in the degree of product differentiation that occurs makes the loss of economic welfare resulting from the imposition of the antitrust rule less than it would have been otherwise. For example, a restriction of size of firm in the industry *may* lead to an increase in the percentage of total costs represented by benign advertising. If it does, a second antitrust rule that restricts advertising expenditures by firms will only bring about a further reduction in economic welfare.

5 · UNACCEPTABLE PRODUCT DIFFERENCES. The poor quality of economic analysis applied to the phenomenon of product variety since the youth of Edward Chamberlin is rather disheartening given the enormous number of words that have been devoted to it.[10] Still, the most plausible explanation of why economists have not done better is not entirely discreditable to us. It is simply that we have allowed an honorable distaste for certain forms of product differentiation to overcome scientific caution. This has been especially true when advertising, the most discussed though not necessarily the most important form of product differentiation, is involved.[11] An advertising campaign designed to promote peppermint-flavored aspirin as a cure for cancer would be unspeakably horrible. The "efficiency" of the processes by which such a product was manufactured and advertised would be supremely unimportant. The main difficulty for economists is that a judgment that some particular form of product differentiation is *mala in se* cannot be made within the context of axiomatic economic theory where consumer utility functions are "given" and an acceptable goal of policy is taken as the maximization of a social welfare function derived, at any rate

[10] A recent and notable exception to this severe generalization is D. A. Worcester, Jr., *Monopoly, Big Business, and Welfare in the Postwar United States* (Seattle, Wash., 1967), especially pp. 9–42. Nevertheless, I must dissent from Worcester's decision to equate "bad" product differentiation with that which makes possible price discrimination. The two phenomena are, I believe, economically distinct. Product differentiation involves an increase in the alternatives open to buyers, whereas price discrimination depends upon the sellers' ability to restrict these alternatives by creating or taking advantage of impediments to arbitrage.

[11] In the United States, since 1920, the fraction of national income represented by advertising outlays has been remarkably constant at between 2 and 3 per cent. L. G. Telser, "Some Aspects of the Economics of Advertising," *Journal of Business,* 41 (1968), 166.

in part, from individual utility functions. Such a judgment must be based upon an appeal to other values that cannot be directly implemented through the market.[12]

Three sorts of appeal seem to characterize most criticisms of product variety in the real world. The first, and least controversial, is an appeal to superior information. Most economists have somewhere learned that aspirin in the United States is a homogeneous product; and we not unreasonably assume that, if our fellow consumers had this information, they would not knowingly buy a higher-priced brand if the cheapest brand were available. Hence economists conclude that economic welfare can be increased by outlawing the advertising of aspirin on the assumption that, if nobody told them differently, most consumers would assume that all tablets called aspirin represented the same chemical compound. But the welfare that would be increased by suppressing the advertising of aspirin is not the welfare of "given" utility functions based upon the information that consumers currently possess. It is the welfare

[12] The above remarks on the difficulty of passing judgment on the social utility of product differences mainly echo a point made many years ago by J. M. Cassels. After noting that product differentiations have been criticized because people do not always know how much variety would be good for them and cannot very accurately control their market responses to the variety that is actually given them, Cassels observes: "These are undoubtedly valid criticisms of our economic system and the agreement would be almost unanimous that certain extreme cases of artificial differentiation are distinctly wasteful from the social point of view. But it must be recognized that in the formulation of such judgments we are led almost inevitably to introduce considerations which, according to the usual distinctions, are non-economic in character. If we question the social desirability of having half a dozen competing brands of cigarettes, must we not also be prepared to question in a similar way the desirability of having cigarettes at all, or at least of having them in the quantity that we do have them?" "Excess Capacity and Monopolistic Competition," *Quarterly Journal of Economics,* LI (1937), 438.

of the utility functions that consumers would (presumably) have if they were in possession of the "correct" information.

A second criticism of product variety in the real world is based upon an appeal to superior taste. This criticism is seldom expressed in simple and direct language since it smacks of a condescension that is politically unwise. Nevertheless, many (if not most) cultivated people would favor some effort by the state through education, regulation, and taxation to discourage less elevated consumers from buying television sets mounted in French provincial wood cabinets or cosmetics sold in unstandardized, flossy packages. If the vulgar outnumber the refined among consumers, vulgarity must, of course, be the apparent consequence of product differentiation.

Finally, much criticism of product variety derives from the recognition that there exists a kind of consumer schizophrenia. A nation acting through the market may elect, even after "promotional" or exhortative advertising has been abolished, to sacrifice a certain quantity of medical care, for example, in order to have ten different models of small cars. Yet the same nation using the political process may prefer to restrict consumer choice in automobiles in order to free resources for additional medicine. This kind of consumer schizophrenia is not confined to differentiated products; indeed, it characterizes all economic choice. While the citizen of North Carolina who votes for prohibition in local option elections and then regularly patronizes a bootlegger may exasperate the economist who is trying to deduce his utility function, he is not really behaving irrationally. He may simply believe that all people including himself should be discouraged by the state from drinking and still have no intention of abstaining in the absence of effective coercion. If our citizen is fined $25 for illegal possession of distilled spirits, he alone is capable of saying whether the fine has made him better off (because his respect for law enforcement is increased) or worse off (because his disposable income is reduced).

6 · RECAPITULATION. Product differences can be divided into those which are benign and those which are *mala in se*. Economic analysis which takes consumer tastes as given can be applied only to benign differences. Here it can be employed to establish the conditions under which a set of benignly differentiated products will be produced and marketed at the lowest total cost. Once product differentiation enters the picture, cost and revenue in the firm become functions of other variables besides "output," and the algebra needed to demonstrate equilibrium for the firm and industry becomes much more complicated. Yet the appearance of this phenomenon changes nothing of importance.

The goal of the multiplant firm is still to secure for itself the greatest profit commensurate with the exclusion of other firms from the industry. To achieve this goal it must manufacture and market a set of differentiated products and do so in the most efficient manner. When product differences are, by definition, benign, presumably there is some optimal amount and degree of differentiation. How closely this optimum is approached is a function of the demand for the set of differentiated products and the size of production and marketing units needed to manufacture and differentiate them in the most efficient way.

Whether, in economic analysis, one prefers to stress product variety in the interest of realism or product similarity in order to emphasize certain fundamental truths about price making is a matter of personal taste. My own feeling is that "monopolistic competition" is mainly useful as an antidote to the obsession with equilibrium that the economist must eternally guard against. Once the possibility of product differentiation is admitted, the exploratory character of business activity is underscored and the obstacles to achieving equilibrium, even in the simplest of static models, become more obvious.

Product differences which are *mala in se* can be so classified because they are based upon an exploitation of the consumer's ignorance of the best relevant information, because they reflect what Authority has condemned as bad taste, or because they are incompatible with the use of resources that consumers seek to secure through the political process. Virtually all the important policy issues presented by product differentiation—advertising, trademarks, non-price competition in the form of service and styling, etc.—involve product differences of this second category. Economists *qua* economists have little to say about them except the obvious: for example, that a decision to use the political process in the place of the price system will encourage black markets, whereas too much reliance on markets is likely to lead to civil disorder or worse.

CHAPTER 6 *The Case of Impeded Entry*

1 · IMPEDED ENTRY DEFINED. In Chapter 4 we assigned a rather unusual meaning to the much used but seldom defined term "free entry." We accepted not only that newcomers are legally free and technologically competent to establish themselves in the imperfectly competitive industry. We assumed, in addition, that they would "immediately" enter whenever they could do so without incurring a loss. Our argument for using such an austere definition of free entry was simple but persuasive. It is the only definition of free entry that allows us to determine the equilibrium price and output of an imperfectly competitive industry without concerning ourselves with two exceedingly complicated issues: entrepreneurial tastes for risk and techniques employed by entrepreneurs to appraise risk. Still, while pedagogical simplicity is a legitimate goal in economic analysis, it is certainly not the only goal. Let us now relax the purist's definition of free entry and consider the case where entry is legally free and new firms will have the same access to technology and resources as old firms—but only at some date in the future that cannot be known in advance.

The uncertainty respecting the exact date at which the entry of a newcomer will become economically feasible must be emphasized. If the exact date of entry is known in advance, the correct marketing strategy for the established firm in an imperfectly competitive industry is clear. It can do nothing to prevent the eventual disappearance of its competitive advantage. Therefore in the short run it will behave as if it owns a protected monopoly (and in a sense it does). When its grace period of immunity from competition is nearly over, the established firm will initiate a policy of stay-out pricing, that is, it will begin to produce the output and collect the economic rent of stable equilibrium as defined in Chapter 4. To this end it may itself undertake the necessary expansion of the industry's plant capacity. Or it may cooperate with investors who wish to enter the industry to the end of ensuring that no "unnecessary" plants are built.

Nothing of significance in this analysis is changed if we posit that entry for a new firm has a decreasing cost over time. That is, while entry is certain to occur at some time in the future, the date of economically feasible entry can be brought forward if prospective newcomers are prepared to incur certain costs of research and development. The only effect of this change in our premises is to reduce the length of time during which the established firm behaves as if it were a protected monopoly.

The only really interesting case of impeded entry occurs when the established firm knows that there is a danger that, should its rate of return on capital invested rise above some minimum threshhold level, a new firm may enter the industry, but nevertheless believes that this danger is small enough to make it worthwhile to keep its rate of return above this level. As we know, this case seems to be typical of many industries where the scale of efficient production is large relative to demand. In such a case we ought to acknowledge unequivocally that no stable equilibrium can exist since, every so often, the established firm's gamble will fail and a new firm will enter. When this happens, the game must begin again. Actually there are only two questions about impeded entry that are of interest to economists. The first relates to the strategy (or strategies) that the established firm will adopt in the hope of discouraging entry; the second, to the kinds of instability in the industry that these different strategies imply.

Let us be clear that, if our examination of the case of impeded entry is to produce useful results, we must begin by casting out of our minds some very important parts of the conceptual apparatus that we habitually employ in equilibrium analysis. Above all, we can no longer affirm, at one and the same time, that (a) the demand curve for the industry's product looks the same to the established firm and to a potential newcomer, and that (b) the two rivals have "equal access to technology and resources" or "the same costs of production." When entry is impeded by the fact of uncertainty, one, or both, of these statements must be false. For if they are both true, there is no uncertainty that gives rise to conflicting views of the industry's future profitability. The cost of entering the industry is subject to slide-rule calculation, and the established firm will protect its market position by resorting to a permanent policy of stay-out pricing.

In order for us to imagine a situation in which the established firm chooses to risk the entry of a newcomer by charging more than the "safe" stay-out price, we must assume either that it believes its judgment about the costs of entry to be superior to that of any newcomer or that it is managed by men who are prepared to incur uncertainty in the effort to increase profit. Uncertainty may, of course, pertain to the supply side or the demand side of the market or, for that matter, to both sides. That is, should the established firm elect to gamble on the entry of a newcomer because of what it believes to be its superior judgment, it may do so for one or both of two reasons. It believes that its own managers are better able to predict demand for the industry's product than anybody else's managers. Or it believes them to be better able to estimate the costs that a new firm must incur in order to enter.[1]

To simplify our task of describing the behavior of the established firm in the case of impeded entry, let us make one change in the assumptions employed in the analysis of imperfect competition under static conditions in the preceding chapters. In this chapter we shall assume that the only uncertainty in the industry relates to the cost that a new firm must incur in order to enter the industry. More specifically, the managers of the established firm are presumed to have formed a "personalistic" estimate of this cost, that is, they

---

[1] For pedagogical convenience, in this chapter impeded entry is discussed in terms of the alternative strategies facing an established firm which enjoys no legal monopoly of its market. Robert Sherman and T. D. Willett have recently argued that the price relied upon by the established firm in the hope of discouraging the entry of rivals may actually be lower when it faces only one rival. This result is held to be possible because, when deciding whether or not to enter an apparently profitable industry, a potential entrant may be dissuaded by the knowledge that somebody else may also enter and that, if both enter, the industry will become unprofitable for everyone. The established firm, so the argument goes, may make use of these apprehensions to charge a higher price than it would risk with only one potential entrant to worry about.

Although I do not find this argument persuasive, it certainly describes a logical possibility. (When businessmen are presumed to act upon the basis of incomplete information, almost anything is possible.) The argument, however, does not conflict with the assumptions of this chapter, since we do not seek to go behind the probability coefficients that the manager of the established firm assigns to the possible payoffs of alternative strategies. See Roger Sherman and T. D. Willett, "Potential Entrants Discourage Entry," *Journal of Political Economy,* LXXV (1967), 400–403.

have satisfied themselves that certain outcomes are possible and have assigned a probability coefficient to each possible outcome. Investors who explore the attractions of organizing a new firm in the industry are presumed to form their own, different, personalistic estimates of the cost of entry. Thus the decision of an investment group to challenge an established firm signifies only one thing. It believes that the managers of the established firm have exaggerated the cost of entry, and it is willing to back this opinion by risking a certain quantity of capital.

Note that when we set up the problem in this way, all investors are presumed to have identical attitudes toward uncertainty. Hence, should an investment group challenge the established firm and fail ignominiously, it goes down to defeat because its information was grossly inaccurate, not because it took "foolish" chances. Conversely, when the new firm goes forward to outstanding success, we must infer that the prosperity gained is a function of managerial wisdom rather than managerial luck on a foolhardy gamble.

2 · THE USES OF EXCESS CAPACITY. A convenient jumping-off place for a discussion of the case of impeded entry is offered by Figure 6-1. Demand for the industry's product is given by DD', and marginal revenue curve by DM. The industry is assumed to be in the hands of an established firm that owns three plants. Unit cost for this firm is given by the kinked curve UU', and marginal cost by the three discontinuous curves that intersect UU'.

Let us assume that in Figure 6-1 the established firm behaves as if demand is given by DD' and unit cost for its three plants by UU'. Let us assume also that it believes that:

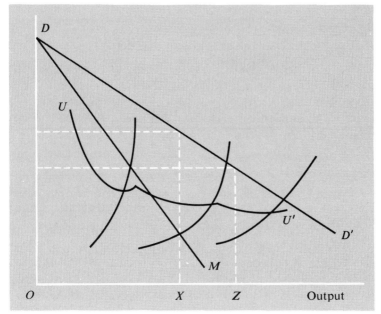

Figure 6-1

1. There is a probability of 1.0 (unity) that newcomers will not enter the industry provided that the established firm (a) remains in a position to operate three plants and (b) uses them to produce output *OZ*.

2. There is a zero probability that newcomers will stay out of the industry if less than three plants are maintained whatever the output produced (because an output in the neighborhood of *OZ* would be inefficiently produced if only one or two plants were used).

3. When three plants are maintained in existence, the probability that a new firm will enter is 1.0 (unity) provided that output *OX* is produced.

4. When three plants are maintained in existence, and an output between *OX* and *OZ* is produced, the probability that

a new firm will be drawn into the industry is greater than zero but less than unity.

These four assumptions dictate the following conclusion: The established firm, provided that it is willing to incur some risk in return for the chance to increase profit, will produce an output equal to, or greater than, OX but less than OZ. The intriguing question is: What factors govern the probability that a new firm will enter the industry? Two are clearly implicit in the above discussion: (a) the amount of plant capacity that the established firm has in existence, and (b) the current profit of the established firm. These two factors can be easily identified and quantified. A third factor is the potential entrant's estimate of what use the established firm will make of its excess capacity when its market position is threatened. This factor, unfortunately, is not so easily quantified. We can only assume that how it is assessed by the potential entrant bears some relation to the past behavior of the established firm—that he is more likely to challenge an established firm with a reputation for bluffing than one with a reputation for fighting long and costly economic wars. (The subject of economic warfare is sufficiently difficult, ill-defined, and riddled with misconceptions that we consider it in detail in Chapter 7.)

3 · THE CHOICE OF A STRATEGY. The strategy problem that faces the established firm in the case of impeded entry is, of course, exceedingly complex because its solution requires a number of decisions, each of which can have more than one possible outcome. In this chapter we attempt only to structure the problem—to borrow a favorite phrase of sociologists. This can be done with the aid of Figure 6-2 which contains the set of logical possibilities.

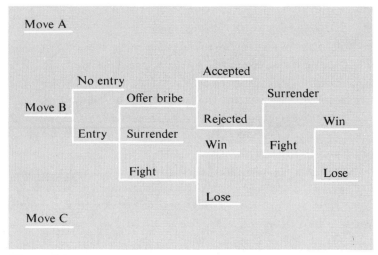

Figure 6-2

Every output between *OX* and *OZ* in Figure 6-1 can be viewed as a separate and distinct initial "move" in an economic war between established firm and challenger. Each of these moves will either succeed or fail. Let there be three possible outputs greater than *OX* but less than *OZ*. Let them be represented by moves A, B, and C in Figure 6-2. (Thus move A might correspond to an output slightly greater than *OX*, and move C to an output slightly less than *OZ*.)

A move is successful if another firm does not undertake to enter the industry. A move is a failure if a threat of entry does develop. Should the first move of the established firm suffice to discourage the entry of another firm, nothing more need be said. The war game, so to speak, is decided in one play. Should the first move not suffice to block entry, the established firm must make another move which, like the first, will either succeed or fail. As Figure 6-2 indicates, when the first move fails, the established firm is presented with three alternatives.

1. It may capitulate and minimize loss by entering into a profit-sharing cartel with the challenger.

2. It may offer a bribe to the challenger payable on condition that the challenger give up his effort to enter the industry. This move must, of course, be made before the challenger has completed the investment needed to begin production.

3. It may declare war on the challenger and, by a policy of price cutting or greater expenditures for advertising, seek to drive him from the industry.

A decision by the established firm to capitulate after the first move has failed to exclude the challenger will end the war game. So also will the offer and acceptance of a bribe. If the decision of the established firm, either before or after the offer of a bribe, is to fight, the game goes on; and it continues until the challenger is either driven from the industry or is accepted by the established firm into a profit-sharing cartel. As Figure 6-2 indicates, eight possible outcomes are associated with the business conflict set in motion by every initial move. One outcome represents total success for the established firm, three outcomes represent partial success, and four outcomes signify failure.

The set of logical possibilities described in Figure 6-2 can serve as the basis for a number of different war games, each one corresponding to the set rules which the established firm adopts in choosing its strategy. For purposes of illustration we shall confine our attention to the simplest type of game, one wherein the complete sequence of moves is decided upon before the game begins.

Let us assume that the officer of the established firm in charge of war plans mentally constructs a payoff table for each move in the game and assigns a probability coefficient to each possible outcome. He must then rank all possible strategies according to some set of rules. But, what set of rules? The choice is dictated by the officer's attitude toward uncertainty. He will, of course, view the utility of any given strategy as a function of two variables: its expected value, and the dispersion of its possible outcomes. Let us make the reasonable assumption that the officer in charge of war planning is a judicious profit maximizer in that, in choosing his strategy, he follows two rules. First, he prefers every strategy with a higher expected value to one with a lower expected value. Second, if two (or more) strategies have the same expected value, he will (following good game theory) select the one which promises him the highest minimum gain.

In the business situation depicted by Figure 6-2 the officer of the established firm who wishes to discourage the entry of a new firm into the industry can choose from a set of twelve possible strategies. He can produce three possible outputs; and the decision to produce any one of them can set in motion four different strategies. For example, when the initial decision is to "play B," the following alternatives are present.

B1. Play B. If it fails, surrender; that is, enter into a profit-sharing cartel with the challenger.
B2. Play B. If it fails, offer bribe. If bribe is rejected, surrender.
B3. Play B. If it fails, offer bribe. If bribe is rejected, fight.
B4. Play B. If it fails, do not offer bribe but declare war immediately.

Note that strategies B1, B2, B3, and B4 do not have the same number of possible outcomes. Thus, when strategy B1 is followed, two outcomes are possible. (a) The established firm plays B and no other firm attempts to enter the industry. (b) Alternatively, the established firm plays B, a new firm attempts to enter, and the established firm thereupon surrenders.

Strategy C3			
Outcome (π)	Probability (p)	$E(\pi)$ (πp)	$E(S)$ $(\Sigma \pi p)$
40	0.3	12	
35	0.3	10.5	
			24.9
12	0.2	2.4	
0	0.2	0	

Table 6-1

When strategy B3 is followed, however, four outcomes are possible. (a) The established firm plays B, and no new firm attempts to enter. (b) It plays B, a new firm attempts to enter, and the established firm offers a bribe which is accepted. (c) The established firm plays B, a new firm attempts to enter, a bribe is offered and rejected, and the established firm fights and wins. (d) When its bribe is rejected, the established firm fights and loses.

The expected value of every strategy is, of course, obtained by multiplying the value of each possible outcome by its probability coefficient and taking the sum of the products. Table 6-1 provides the relevant information on strategy C3

Strategy									$E(S)$
A1	60	$\frac{1}{10}$	10	$\frac{9}{10}$					15
A2	60	$\frac{1}{10}$	40	$\frac{3}{10}$	5	$\frac{6}{10}$			21
A3	60	$\frac{1}{10}$	40	$\frac{3}{10}$	30	$\frac{3}{10}$	0	$\frac{3}{10}$	27
A4	60	$\frac{1}{10}$	46	$\frac{5}{10}$	0	$\frac{4}{10}$			29
B1	55	$\frac{2}{10}$	10	$\frac{8}{10}$					19
B2*	55	$\frac{2}{10}$	45	$\frac{2}{10}$	15	$\frac{6}{10}$			29
B3	55	$\frac{2}{10}$	45	$\frac{2}{10}$	25	$\frac{3}{10}$	0	$\frac{3}{10}$	27.5
B4	55	$\frac{2}{10}$	30	$\frac{4}{10}$	0	$\frac{4}{10}$			23
C1	40	$\frac{3}{10}$	10	$\frac{7}{10}$					19
C2	40	$\frac{3}{10}$	35	$\frac{3}{10}$	5	$\frac{4}{10}$			24.5
C3	40	$\frac{3}{10}$	35	$\frac{3}{10}$	12	$\frac{2}{10}$	0	$\frac{2}{10}$	24.9
C4	40	$\frac{3}{10}$	30	$\frac{4}{10}$	0	$\frac{3}{10}$			24

*Preferred strategy.

Table 6-2

with its four possible outcomes. The expected value of C3 is $(40 \times 0.3) + (35 \times 0.3) + (12 \times 0.2) + (0 \times 0.2)$ or 24.9.

Table 6-2 provides all the information needed for a preference ranking of the twelve strategies open to the established firm which seeks to discourage the entry of a new firm by forgoing some part of its monopoly profit. In each diagonally

divided box of Table 6-2 the value of an outcome is given
in the upper left corner. The probability that this outcome will
occur is given in the lower right corner of the box. The expected value of each strategy is given in the column desig-
nated $E(S)$.

We have posited that the officer in charge of war planning
in the established firm will follow two rules when choosing his
strategy. He will select the strategy that has the greatest expected value. If the maximum expected value attaches to two or
more different strategies, he will select the one that ensures
the highest minimum gain. Following these rules, and presented
with the information contained in Table 6-2, he must choose
strategy B2, which has an expected value of 29 and a minimum
payoff of 15.

4 · A PERSPECTIVE ON IMPEDED ENTRY. If the
potential entrant believes that his entry into the industry
is certain to provoke the established firm to retaliate by putting
excess capacity to work come hell or high water, he will, of
course, stay out. For if this be his view, he can only conclude
that his entry would make the industry unprofitable for both
the established firm and himself.

In the example of impeded entry discussed above, however,
the potential entrant can have no such expectation. This must
be so because he knows that the established firm is managed
by sensible men. The challenger may suspect that the established firm is prepared to incur certain costs in order to exclude him from the industry and hence will not immediately
surrender—that is, agree to join with him in a profit-sharing
cartel—as soon as he appears on the scene. He may also
believe that the established firm has underestimated the costs
needed to defeat his bid to enter. Indeed, as we have seen,

when challenger and established firm are presumed to have the same attitude toward uncertainty, the challenger must believe that the established firm has underestimated these costs before he will decide to enter.

In this connection we might note that the strategies of both contestants may, or may not, contain an element of bluff, a bluff being possible whenever one side can conceal its intended strategy from the other. When concealment can be practiced, the established firm may publicly proclaim that it will seek to crush a challenger, if necessary by a costly price war, while privately resolving to capitulate as soon as a serious threat of entry materializes. Certain strategies are serviceable even though the intent to use them is disclosed in advance; but clearly those strategies which rule out the actual use of excess capacity to carry on a price war are not of this type. (In our example the non-fighting strategies are A1, A2, B1, B2, C1, C2.) Should the established firm, however, intend to employ a strategy that does not exclude the possibility of a price war, the utility of such a strategy is not destroyed, although it may be diminished, by the disclosure of intent.

In our example, when the established firm really means to follow strategy A4, B4, or C4 (fight as soon as a challenge is received), it has every incentive to proclaim its determination. When it means to use strategy A3, B3, or C3 (offer a bribe and go to war only if bribe declined), the utility of the strategy is reduced but not wholly eliminated by an information leak.

We might pause here to reiterate again the assumption that we introduced earlier in order to make possible a duel of wits between established firm and challenger. It is that the managers of the established firm believe that the challenger has underestimated the cost that must be incurred to enter the industry. This assumption suffices to create a case of impeded entry. When the established firm and challenger are presumed to base their price-output decisions on the same set of rules— that is, when both are presumed to have the same "utility function"—it is the indispensable assumption.

Nevertheless, let us be clear that this chapter has considered only one case of impeded entry. Another possibility would arise if we reversed the above assumptions. That is, we could get impeded entry by allowing the established firm and the challenger to make their price-output decision on the basis of the same cost estimates (cost being viewed as a random variable) but giving the challenger the greater penchant for gambling.

There is not much to be gained by pursuing this will-he-or-won't-he type of speculation in great detail. Although the history of American business is only a small part of world business history, it contains vastly more examples of techniques used by established firms to protect a market position than the mind of the most inventive economist could ever imagine. The bribe not to enter the industry has been paid in a hundred different ways over the years: in the purchase of patents; with seats on the established firm's board of directors; in consultants' fees; in the purchase of half-finished plants at "inflated" values; and with assurances that the challenger will be helped by the established firm to undertake the penetration of some other industry. The techniques employed in the attempt to crush a rival who could not be bribed (or who was not worth bribing) have ranged from an increase in the advertising budget of the established firm to the Saint Valentine's Day massacre in Al Capone's Chicago. And when one side or both have wearied of economic war, the formal or informal agreements that have reestablished peace have made almost every possible division of monopoly profit between established firm and challenger. But we shall not pursue this matter further. The intricacies and complexities of economic warfare is a subject that can more profitably be explored by business historians than by economic theorists.

There is an even better reason for declining to worry at great length about the behavior of established firm and challenger in the case of impeded entry. Provided that the established firm learns from experience and dislikes uncertainty, its output over any extended period will not average more than OZ in Figure 6-1. (Recall that OZ is the output which the established firm believes would make certain the exclusion of a rival.) For should its output over any extended period exceed OZ, the attempt at a sophisticated strategy would obviously be irrational. The established firm would stand to increase its profit by producing a steady output OZ and removing the threat of entry once and for all.[2]

5 · IMPEDED ENTRY AS A RAISON D'ÊTRE FOR ANTITRUST. One other result worth emphasizing emerges from our consideration of the case of impeded entry. Over the years some economists have deplored the magnitude of the American antitrust effort devoted to harassing cartels on the ground that cartels are inherently unstable. This instability is held to be present for one or both of two reasons.

[2] Thus the leading history of the Standard Oil Company implies that, in the 1880s, the most famous of trusts was moved by experience to substitute a form of stay-out pricing for the previously favored strategy that involved the intimidation and purchase of rivals. The correspondence of John D. Rockefeller and his partners indicates that, by 1890, they had come to believe that the probability that newcomers would enter the industry was a function of the trust's price policy; and that, in the past, the trust had erred in making the industry too tempting to what Rockefeller called blackmailers. Allan Nevins, *Study in Power: John D. Rockefeller, Industrialist and Philanthropist* (New York, 1953), Vol. II, pp. 60–75.

A cartel, it is alleged, is likely to contain at least one chiseler whose obtuseness or rashness will cause the failure of any joint venture to restrict output. And to the extent that chiseling can be suppressed or at least reduced to proportions that make the cartel economically viable, its profits will draw new firms into the industry and so cause its collapse.

It is true that cartels are unstable. Yet it is equally true that, in a world of free contract, the uncoordinated rivalry of any group of imperfect competitors is also unstable. In such a laissez-faire world, one would expect that, most of the time, most industries would operate subject to some type of cartel control. For, to say the obvious, it always pays the members of an industry to invest in cartel formation as long as cartel benefits exceed cartel costs and—let us not forget—as long as the member firms are satisfied that the net gain realized from cartel formation does not "unduly" increase the danger that new firms will be drawn into the industry.

It is really the "fact" of impeded entry in the real world that provides the principal justification that economic theory can offer for antitrust restrictions on cartels and mergers. We found in Chapter 4 that, when entry is free in the sense of being an instantaneous possibility, there exists a strong presumption that such restrictions reduce economic welfare. On this assumption they *must* serve to increase unit cost of production by preventing the most efficient use of whatever plant capacity is in existence; they *may* serve to reduce the industry's output as well.

To the extent that entry into the industry is impeded by uncertainty respecting the cost of entry, restrictions on mergers and cartels can increase output by bringing about the use of plant capacity that would otherwise remain idle. This is merely a generalization of the proposition developed in Chapter 3 about the merits of monopoly and no-entry oligopoly.

There we found that, when entry is totally impeded (impossible) and aggregate demand fluctuates over time, industry output may be greater (and cannot be less) when the industry is organized as an oligopoly than when it is organized as a monopoly. However, in the case of impeded entry as in the case of no-entry oligopoly, the greater output obtained by enforcing antitrust rules will not be produced in the technically most efficient manner. The addition to economic welfare of the incremental output may be greater than the welfare loss associated with technically inefficient production. Then, again, it may not.[3] The most we can say is that the arguments for restricting mergers and cartels which are derived from static economic theory are most relevant to industries where entry is impeded.

[3] On this tradeoff problem see O. E. Williamson, "Economies as an Antitrust Defence," *American Economic Review*, LVIII (1968), 18–36.

CHAPTER 7

Economic Warfare

1 · SOME AMBIGUITIES. Over the years, economists, especially in the United States, have been intermittently concerned with an ill-defined business phenomenon that is variously called "unfair competition," "predatory competition," "cutthroat competition," and "economic warfare." This last description has been favored by Europeans, while Americans have been inclined to use the more emotionally laden term "unfair competition." This terminological difference is not without interest, for it suggests what, in fact, has been the case. European writers have usually viewed economic warfare as a not-too-important type of business behavior which is capable of dispassionate analysis. To many American economists such behavior is both important (or, at any rate, would be important if it were not repressed by antitrust laws) and thoroughly obnoxious. We might say that the unfair competition of American economists equals economic warfare plus the observer's condemnation.

The problem of identifying unfair competition is further complicated by the fact that, in the United States, the term denotes a much wider range of behavior to lawyers and laymen than it does to economists. Indeed, any small businessman who has lost out in the competitive struggle to a larger rival is likely to believe that *ipso facto* he is a victim of unfair competition. If only to preserve his self-respect, he is loath to concede that he may have suffered defeat because the greater size of his rival conferred economies of scale that he could not match.

Again, American lawyers and laymen generally brand as unfair competition business practices which they believe to be unethical or immoral regardless of the effect of such practices on market structure. The tactic of bribing the employee of a business rival to betray his trust is almost universally viewed as unfair competition. Yet an insensitive economist could point out that, although commercial bribery may be bad for the souls of men, it may well contribute to the efficiency of the competitive process in at least two ways: by exacerbating the suspicions that rival businessmen entertain for one another, and by speeding up the dissemination of business information.

In the United States, economists seem first to have become interested in unfair competition during the era of the trusts (roughly 1890–1910) when in a great number of industries (approximately sixty-five) a single firm came to produce 60 per cent or more of total national output.[1] The early history of the Standard Oil Company was widely thought to contain many instances of tactics which were unfair in the sense of being socially wasteful. The annals of the National Cash Register Company were also believed to provide horrendous examples of unfair competition; and, in one of Learned Hand's most famous decisions, the Corn Products Refining Company was soundly castigated for the zeal with which it sought to eliminate competitors in the cornstarch and glucose markets.[2]

---

[1] R. L. Nelson, *Merger Movements in American Industry: 1895–1956* (Princeton, N.J., 1959), p. 102.

[2] One passage in Learned Hand's opinion in the Corn Products case contains the best statement of what economists seems to have in mind

Writing in 1912, J. B. Clark and the young J. M. Clark even went so far as to identify unfair competition as a major cause of monopoly in the American economy.

There are, as we have seen, certain ways, nearly all now well known, in which a trust can crush an efficient competitor—the man who is producing goods cheaply and who normally ought to survive. It may make use of the "factor's agreement" by which it gives a special rebate to those merchants who handle only its own goods. It may resort, secondly, to the familiar plan of cutting prices locally—entering its rival's special territory and selling goods there below the cost of producing them, while sustaining itself by means of higher prices charged in other portions of its field. Again, the trust may depend on the cutting of the price of some one variety of goods which a rival producer makes, in order to ruin him, while it sustains itself by means of the high prices

when they speak of unfair competition that I have come across. Let the reader note, however, that the apparent sophistication of Hand's remarks is deceptive. He eloquently condemns the defendant for having attempted to destroy certain competitors. But this condemnation is made to rest on the assertion (not even elaborated with a perfunctory defense) that soft competition, which claims its victims slowly, produces a more efficient use of economic resources than does hard competition, which claims them quickly. According to Hand: "The national will has not declared against the elimination of competitors when they fail from their inherent weakness. On the contrary, it has declared with great emphasis against any methods by which such weakness might be concealed; in so doing it has assumed a positive purpose toward industry, has established a norm to which competition must conform. This purpose the Corn Products Refining Company has persistently and ingeniously endeavored to thwart from the outset. Its constant effort has been to prevent competitors from that test which would in the long run discover they could manufacture as well and as cheaply as itself. It has tried throughout, by its power temporarily to affect commercial conditions, so to obscure the actual industrial facts as to make impossible any test of relative strength. That it has failed does not change the past nor make its continued existence in any sense less compromising to the future." *United States v. Corn Products Refining Co.*, 234 Fed. 964 at 1015 (S. D. N.Y., 1916).

which it gets for goods of other kinds. These three things alone are enough to make the position of a competitor perilous, and they are such important features of monopolistic strategy that the suppression of them would go far toward rescuing competition, protecting the public and insuring to it a large share of the benefit that comes from economies in production.[3]

As we noted above, the economist usually declines to view as unfair competition the defeat of small inefficient firms by large efficient firms or the use of what industry spokesmen regard as unethical trade practices. He is also disinclined to stretch the term to cover two business situations that, on the surface, closely resemble "true" unfair competition (assuming, for the sake of argument, that the phenomenon really exists). The first is the case where a fall in demand or too much investment has created excess capacity in an industry to the extent that two or more firms find themselves operating plants in which output is so low that marginal cost is falling. In this case, production cannot be technically efficient unless some of the industry's plants are shut down; and, when some of the firms have only one plant and profit sharing is illegal or otherwise impossible, competition will rationalize production by forcing some of the one-plant firms to leave the industry. The fact that the firms that are so eliminated may be as efficient as those that survive is irrelevant. But, of course, it may easily be taken by casual observation as an indictment of the process by which winners are separated from losers. The possibility that, in this world, business success or failure can be simply a matter of luck is difficult for most of us to accept.

The second case easily mistaken for "true" unfair competition occurs when a businessman gives way to a sadistic desire to humble a rival even though he must sacrifice income in

---

[3] *The Control of Trusts* (New York, rev. ed., 1912), pp. 96–97.

order to do it. No doubt, such incidents are statistically insignificant; indeed, as one Scottish judge has observed, a case of "mere malicious purpose" must occur seldom if at all in business transactions.[4] Yet incidents which suggest a substantial degree of non-economic sadism (very possibly a manifestation of mental illness) are not unknown and have received attention out of all proportion to their importance.

So much for what unfair competition is not in the lexicon of technical economics. What is it? Since unfair competition can be equated with the type of economic warfare that reduces social welfare, let us seek a definition obliquely by first identifying economic warfare. This is easily done since, by common consent, the price cutting that constitutes economic warfare is distinguished from the price variations associated with "normal" competition in two ways. The price cutting of economic warfare is specific: it is employed by the aggressor firm for the express purpose of injuring a particular rival.[5] And such price cutting is temporary: sooner or later it will either be terminated in a tacit or formal agreement negotiated by the warring parties, or one party will drive the other from the field. In the last case the victor claims whatever spoils have survived the war by raising price and/or lowering the quality of service. Let us be clear that both of these ingredients are needed to transform "normal" competition into economic warfare. Should an oligopolist in say, the mouse-trap industry succeed in devising a patented machine that radically reduces the cost of mouse traps, he may proceed to quote a low price that

---

[4] *Scottish Co-operative Wholesale Society Ltd. v. Glasgow Fleshers' Trade Defence Ass'n.*, 35 S.L. Rep. 645, 651 (1898).

[5] Every instance of allegedly unfair competition cited in one well-known old book involved the use of tactics aimed at a specific competitor. W. H. S. Stevens, *Unfair Competition* (Chicago, 1917), especially pp. 10–53.

will eventually drive his rivals out of business. But since some part of the price reduction will be permanent (the fortunate manufacturer having acquired a new and better production function) his price cutting is not economic war. Again, in an industry with many sellers, a firm may experiment with lower prices in order to gain information about demand and cost without intending to injure any particular rival, even though the experimentation necessarily requires that somebody be hurt. Clearly, no hard-and-fast line can be drawn to separate economic warfare from "normal" business rivalry, but the distinction is not, for this reason, without utility.[6]

2 · NO ECONOMIC WARFARE IN THE STATIC CASE. Until perhaps ten years ago most economists would have agreed that:

Where two firms are of approximately equal size and efficiency, and possessed of nearly equal resources, the cutting of price is an inevitable part of the competitive struggle and likely to leave surviving the stronger, and thus usually the more efficient, of the two. But where the two competing firms are of very unequal size and financial strength, the drastic cutting of prices will almost certainly lead to the extinction of the smaller, and not necessarily the potentially less efficient, of the two firms. For the smaller is unlikely to be competing with equal intensity throughout the whole area of the market, or throughout the whole range of products of the larger. A drastic cut of price by the larger firm in some small part of its territory will thus greatly injure the smaller competitor, while leaving the larger able to earn monopoly profits elsewhere.[7]

[6] Some rule-of-thumb tests for distinguishing normal business behavior from economic warfare are offered in R. C. Brooks, Jr., "Price Cutting and Monopoly Power," *Journal of Marketing,* XXV, 5 (1961), 44–49.

[7] E. A. G. Robinson, *Monopoly* (London, 1941), p. 74.

Nowadays not a few economists (including virtually all recent graduates in economics at the University of Chicago) would dispute the above assertions. The history of American business provides innumerable instances of economic warfare; but only in recent years has it become clear that such conflicts have no place in the static economic theory that economists have long favored. Given the assumptions employed in this kind of economics, the use of price cutting to injure a specific business rival is simply irrational conduct. This truth is virtually self-evident in the case where (a) the cost of building an optimum-sized plant is the same for a newcomer as for an established firm; (b) entry is free in the sense of being instantaneous whenever the newcomer can enter without incurring a loss; and (c) there are no antitrust-type restrictions on freedom of contract. As we saw in Chapter 4, on these assumptions, when stable equilibrium is reached the industry will consist of only one firm. Admittedly, the firm in this stable equilibrium will maintain a price low enough to discourage the entry of other producers, but this low price is neither temporary nor directed at anybody in particular. Stay-out pricing *is* the competitive process in operation.

But suppose that, although entry is truly free, the imperfectly competitive industry still approximates one of the many possible tangency solutions; that is, suppose that it has not yet shaken down into stable equilibrium. Will not disequilibrium in imperfect competition be characterized by some form of economic warfare? The answer is still no. As long as production in the industry is technically inefficient, it will pay somebody to undertake its rationalization; but this end can be achieved most cheaply with the aid of mergers and cartels, since the "fact" of technical inefficiency ensures that rationalization can make every member of the industry better off without making any member worse off. The waging of economic war in order to rationalize the industry would simply impose unnecessary costs on victor and vanquished alike—costs which can be avoided provided that everyone behaves sensibly.

We can give the same answer in the disequilibrium case where a change in technology or government policy suddenly throws up a barrier against the entry of new firms in an industry where none had existed before. The firms already established in the industry have an obvious incentive to restrict output and/or rationalize production—moves that may require the shutting of one or more plants. Yet, here again, the transition to a profit-maximizing output can be most cheaply carried out by a policy of production coordination and profit sharing.

In short, given the assumptions usually employed in static economic theory, we draw the following inferences. First, it does not pay to cut price in order to eliminate a rival from the market unless, having taken over his share of the market, one can (a) proceed to increase profit by restricting and/or rationalizing production without (b) having the greater profit act as the magnet that immediately draws new firms into the industry. Second, if such a maneuver is possible, the intelligent (profit-maximizing) course of action is to merge with the rival or join him in a profit-sharing cartel.[8] The conclusion is inescapable: to study economic warfare, we have to relax the assumptions of static economic theory.

At first glance it might seem to be possible to generate an economic war in an otherwise static model by dropping the premise that there are no antitrust-type restrictions on freedom of contract. In a world of free contract which allows free reign

[8] For two of the pioneer attacks on the idea of unfair competition based upon assumptions of static economic theory, see W. A. Leeman, "The Limitations of Local Price-Cutting as a Barrier to Entry," *Journal of Political Economy,* LXIV (1956), 329–34; and J. S. McGee, "Predatory Price Cutting: The Standard Oil (N.J.) Case," *Journal of Law and Economics,* I (1958), 137–69.

to the use of mergers and cartels to rationalize production, the use of economic warfare is perforce irrational. It is not the least-cost way of promoting rationalization. But, if the optimal solution requiring the use of cartels or mergers is ruled out, does not economic warfare become a second-best solution? Have we not here a simple case of profit maximization subject to constraint? Again the answer is no. We shall find presently that, when certain other assumptions of static economic theory are relaxed, a ban on mergers and cartels may increase the probability of economic war. By itself, however, the imposition of antitrust-type restrictions on freedom of contract will not have this effect.

There is, after all, no point in sacrificing short-run earnings in order to drive a rival producer out of business unless, when the victory has been won, one can either acquire his plant at less than replacement cost or ensure that it does not fall into the hands of a third party who will use it to enter the industry. Without such a guarantee it does not pay to cut price in order to destroy the rival, even though the legal code allows no other method of getting rid of him. If one has to pay the defeated rival "fair market value" for his plant—the sum of discounted incomes that it will earn during its remaining life—the victory that eliminated the rival has cost too much. Assuming that the rival is economically rational, one could have obtained his plant at any time by simply paying fair market value and so avoided the expenses of an economic war. If the plant of the defeated rival passes into the hands of a third party, the battle must be fought all over again.

3 · UNCERTAINTY AS A CAUSE OF ECONOMIC WARFARE. In our search for the conditions that can give rise to economic warfare, we come at last to the case of

impeded entry. As we found in Chapter 6, the essence of impeded entry is uncertainty associated with the process by which the profit of an established firm will draw a new firm into the industry. If the established firm knows that its profits will immediately attract new competition, it will charge the stay-out price associated with stable equilibrium. Conversely, if it knows that its profits will not attract new competition until some time in the future, it will charge the same price as would a protected monopolist until the day of reckoning arrives. The established firm faces a strategy decision only when it is uncertain about how potential rivals will react to its moves.

We noted in Chapter 6 that the probability of a new firm entering the industry could be treated as a function of three variables: (a) the established firm's current profit; (b) the amount of excess capacity being maintained by the established firm; and (c) its record of making use of this excess capacity whenever threatened by the entry of a new firm. Thus, the lower the established firm's present profit, the greater the amount of excess capacity that it maintains, and the blacker its reputation for ruthlessness, the smaller is the probability that a new firm will presume to offer a challenge.

However, as we found in Chapter 6, for the case of impeded entry to arise in the first place, one or both of two conditions must be present. There must exist a difference of opinion between the established firm and the challenger respecting the costs of entry and/or the established firm and the challenger must have different tastes for risk. (Recall that in Chapter 6 we confined our attention to the situation where the sole cause of impeded entry was a difference of opinion respecting the costs of entry.) In the event that established firm and challenger estimate the cost of entry in precisely the same way and have precisely the same taste for risk, an exact calculation is possible: at the price set by the established firm, either the challenger will enter the industry or he will not. And the established firm maximizes long-run profit by making sure that the price is set low enough to discourage entry.

In this connection we might reiterate the burden of the last chapter. In the absence of antitrust-type restrictions on freedom of contract, a policy of experimental aggression or probing action may be economically feasible. That is, when a new firm begins to organize in order to enter the industry, the established firm may first seek to bribe the promoters to desist. If the bribe is rejected, the established firm may retaliate by cutting price to a very low level (e.g., to a figure below average variable cost) for some limited period of time. If the challenger withdraws from the industry within this period, the established firm can breathe easier and raise price to a profitable level once more. If the challenger persists, the established firm can negotiate a merger or profit-sharing cartel with him. Thus the economic war merely decides whether the established firm or the new firm has come closer to estimating the latter's cost of entry.

The situation is not much changed if we assume that cartels and mergers are illegal. The only difference is that, *ceterus paribus,* the established firm will maintain the economic war a little longer, since now the alternative to fighting is the acceptance of some variety of duopoly without profit sharing. But clearly the economic war must finally end in victory or defeat for the defender or in his compromise with the challenger.

4 · THE ALLEGED UNFAIRNESS OF ECONOMIC WARFARE. As long as some uncertainty exists respecting the conditions under which a new firm will enter an industry already preempted by an established firm, economic warfare

will always be a logical possibility. Does it follow that such conflict is socially wasteful in that it permits the destruction of small firms that are as efficient as a larger rival? In the language of J. M. Clark, does it follow that the waging of economic war is unfair competition? This question is not merely difficult to answer; our ingenuity is stretched even to devise techniques that would allow us to find an answer even if we had the money and research manpower needed to put them to use.

We note immediately that we cannot answer the question by appealing to the "facts" of business history. If a new firm endures an economic war and successfully establishes itself in the industry, the war has done no harm that can be measured statistically. (The most we can say is that the war may have discouraged other firms from trying to enter the industry in the future.) If the new firm goes down to defeat, it may well have failed because it was inefficient. Nor can any confidence be placed in the argument that economic welfare would be increased if new firms were given some protection against economic war during the early months or years of their operation. This is so even though there is a strong presumption that most new firms, in the beginning, have higher unit costs than most old firms in the same industry; and that at least some of the new firms will ultimately be able to produce as efficiently as the old firms if they are not assailed by "excessive" price cutting during the learning period.

Sympathy for the new firm forced to fight for its life generally ignores the role of the capital market in directing investment. Presumably the inefficiency of the new firm during its early days in the industry is taken into account when the investment decision to organize it is made. No doubt, a public policy which placed curbs on the price policies (or advertising budgets) of established firms could make life easier for new firms. But to the extent that investors are competent to ascertain their own best interests, such a policy would be economically wasteful. It would place a constraint on the use of stay-out pricing, preclude complete rationalization of the industry, and so permit the excess capacity of the Robinson-Chamberlin equilibrium.

The case for protecting new firms against economic warfare waged by established firms is based upon precisely the same error found in the ancient argument that infant domestic industries should be given tariff protection against foreign competition at least until industrial puberty is reached. Such a protectionist policy, so the argument goes, would enable some firms to gain the strength needed for permanent survival. The policy may very well have this result; indeed, whenever a new firm "learns by doing" (which is usually the case), it is likely to have this result. Nevertheless, the fact that a policy of tariff protection has brought into existence a set of domestic firms that can now survive without such protection cannot be accepted as evidence that the policy has been an economic success. For to the extent that the capital market is able accurately to estimate the costs of entry, any new firm which, in the absence of tariff protection, could not have lasted long enough to get unit cost low enough for survival did not deserve to survive.[9]

[9] Of course, the social and private costs of entry into an industry may not exactly coincide, as, for example, when the organization of new but short-lived firms provides valuable managerial training ("learning by doing") to men who go on to fame and fortune in other parts of the economy. There is, however, no good reason for believing *a priori* that the social costs of entry are below the private costs in most industries; indeed, not a few economists would assert the contrary. Thus it is widely believed that industrial concentration encourages research because it ensures that a higher fraction of the economic payoff from investment in the creation of new information will accrue to the sponsor.

In the American economy it has long been true that the great majority of all new firms have ceased to exist before their fifth birthday.[10] And economists and others who study the depressing statistics on business mortality often say that these unsuccessful aspirants fail because they are "underfinanced." In one sense this judgment is tautological. By definition, an underfinanced firm is one which fails to get total revenue equal to, or greater than, total variable cost before the investment stake of the organizers is used up. The judgment that most new firms fail because they are underfinanced, however, has the merit of drawing attention to an important truth, namely, that the probability of success in a business venture is some function of the size of the organizer's initial investment stake. Unfortunately, this truth is often used as a basis for two fallacious inferences: (a) most new firms operate under the handicap of an imperfectly organized capital market; and, hence, (b) they would fare better if certain of its imperfections were removed. We cannot rule out the possibility that more perfect capital markets might encourage both the formation and the survival of new firms. But this result is most unlikely.

It is conceivable that, in a particular business situation, nobody except the potential entrant knows how easy it would be to challenge successfully a fat, flabby monopolist; and that, if investors generally were better informed, the potential entrant would have an easier job in raising capital. It is just as conceivable, and far more likely, that the potential entrant has difficulty in raising capital because other prospective in-

[10] Thus one study found that of the approximately 4.3 million firms in operation on January 1, 1955, only one-third were still doing business under the same management four years later. *Small Business Failures,* Senate Report No. 2270, 87th Congress, 2nd Session (1962), p. 3.

vestors are very well informed about the situation. It is true enough that new firms fail because the initial investment stake of their organizers is used up before sales generate enough revenue to cover total variable costs. But this only happens because, at some point, actual and potential investors come to believe that the new firm is unlikely ever to generate enough income to make further investment in it worthwhile.

No doubt, the number of new firms that last beyond the fifth year in the American economy could be increased if public policy were deliberately used to shift capital from old firms to new firms. To the extent that the probability of business success is a function of the initial investment stake this proposition has to be true. But the fact that business mortality could be cut by rigging the capital market in favor of new firms is no proof that business mortality ought to be reduced in this way. The important question is rather: Would the use of some other method of financing new firms, for example, through a government development corporation, give better results than the present method of financing through the private capital market? This is a supremely important question, and how one answers it pretty much determines the role that one would like to see government play in directing capital formation, but it would be foolhardy to seek an answer in the limited scope of this book. Instead, let us be content to confine our attention to a related but distinctly minor issue: Can public policy by outlawing economic warfare promote freedom of entry in imperfectly competitive industries?

Here we must distinguish two policy alternatives. In the first, economic warfare is outlawed but joint maximization of profit through mergers and cartels is permitted. In the second, both economic warfare and joint maximization of profit are outlawed:

Should the first alternative be chosen as public policy, it is at least possible that the entry of new firms will be made easier. There can be no certainty that the policy will have this result, since the established firm may use stay-out pricing to protect its market position. Should both economic warfare and joint maximization be outlawed, then the entry of new firms will almost certainly be discouraged, since now resort to a permanent policy of stay-out pricing is the only defensive option that the established firm has left.

The one way to make certain that an industry will consist of more than one firm is, of course, to ban economic warfare, joint maximization, *and* stay-out pricing. Unhappily, to adopt this course is to ensure that most plants most of the time will operate where unit cost is falling and hence to condemn the industry to technical inefficiency. Once more we forbear to guess whether the loss in technical efficiency imposed by this type of antitrust rule is justified by the improved distribution of resources among industries that it may bring about.

5 · THE INTIMIDATION THESIS. The argument has been advanced that, although it may appear to be cheaper to buy out a troublesome rival than to destroy him by waging economic war, "the destruction of one rival is likely to intimidate many more whereas the purchase of a rival (except at a distress price) may cause others to appear." [11] In our discussion of the case of impeded entry in Chapter 6, we tacitly accepted the accuracy of this assertion but, at the same time, declined to infer from it that such intimidation necessarily involves a sacrifice of economic welfare. The logic of this reluctance ought now to be spelled out.

In the static case where all potential entrants have complete

[11] F. J. Kottke, "Market Entry and the Character of Competition," *Western Economic Journal*, 5 (1966), 24.

information on the cost and demand functions of the industry, intimidation is, of course, uneconomic and hence irrational. The loss that an aggressor would suffer in an economic war can be calculated to as many decimal places as one wishes. It would be common knowledge how much of an investment stake would be needed to dissuade the established firm from fighting. Assuming that the industry could profitably support additional plant capacity, the necessary stake would be supplied by a syndicate of investors. It follows that intimidation can be practiced only when prospective investors have incomplete information about the industry. Specifically, intimidation can be employed only when the aggressor is in a position to conceal the extent of his own wounds suffered in a price war and/or to exaggerate those of his adversary.

Should intimidation be outlawed by the adoption of an antitrust rule, the cost of discouraging the entry of rivals will be raised for the established firm; indeed, this cost may become prohibitive. But here again it does not follow that economic welfare will increase *pari passu* as additional firms guided by inexperienced managers enter the industry. Under conditions of uncertainty, any lowering of the costs of entry into an industry perforce increases the danger that overinvestment will lead to technically inefficient production.

6 · UNFAIR COMPETITION AS A USEFUL MYTH. Our investigation in this chapter has established that, on the assumptions usually employed in static economic theory, there can be no such thing as economic warfare. The prizes that could be claimed by the victor (if any) could be more cheaply gained through mergers or cartels. Yet we have found that, once the assumptions of static economic theory are relaxed to allow for some uncertainty respecting the costs of

organizing a new firm and/or differences in the willingness of businessmen to bear uncertainty, economic warfare is a logical possibility.

Our investigation, however, has also shown that it does not follow that, because economic warfare exists, it is socially wasteful. We have had to reject as irrelevant or inconclusive virtually all the evidence that has been produced over the years that seeks to show how the public is hurt by "unfair competition." The ideological consequences which follow from this rejection are really quite startling—far more so than might appear at first glance. For it is the assumption that there is such a thing as unfair competition that provides one of the major justifications for antitrust policy. In fact, as a matter of intellectual history, American economists had grave doubts about the wisdom of antitrust until, in the early 1900s, they became persuaded that there did exist a form of competition that was both ethically objectionable and socially wasteful. We usually forget that in the 1890s the leading American economists either dismissed the Sherman Act as meaningless or greeted it with suspicion bordering on hostility. In view of their training in classical economic theory and German historicism, this reaction is hardly surprising.[12]

The rise of the large firms compelled the economist, especially in the United States, to engage in some painful rethinking. He had been trained to believe that economic welfare was increased when businessmen were given wide freedom of contract. And his favorite writers (notably Alfred Marshall and John Stuart Mill) assured him that, as long as businessmen enjoyed no legal protection against others who envied their

[12] The generally unhelpful attitude of the leading American economists to antitrust legislation in the 1880s and 1890s is discussed in William Letwin, *Law and Economic Policy in America* (New York, 1965), pp. 71–77.

profits, competition would persist. When he could no longer deny the evidence of his senses that large firms had come to stay, the economist was faced with a painful choice. Given his training, he had to accept that the so-called trusts had prospered because they were technically more efficient than smaller firms. His problem was the interpretation to be placed upon this fact. The economist could infer that the replacement of many small firms by a single large firm in an industry really had no great significance for competition; that the large firm would face the prospect, if not the certainty, of competition should its profit go above the "competitive" level. Hence the rather querulous caution of one nineteenth-century academic: "We must not assume that because competition is not observable in the form seen on the produce exchange, it is not discoverable in any form." [13]

Alternatively, the economist could conclude that the traditional case for competition as a promoter of economic welfare had been subverted by change in technology and was no longer valid. If he drew this inference, he had also to accept the unpalatable truth that the despised socialists had been right all along. Changes in technology really were destroying the preconditions of competition and making inevitable and desirable the concentration of production in large firms.

In short, when the economist of the 1890s turned to his intellectual heritage for guidance on the vociferously discussed trust issues of the day, he found that he had either to ignore trusts or to defend them—and neither alternative greatly appealed to him. From this painful dilemma he was liberated by the immensely convenient doctrine of unfair competition. For if the success of the trusts rested mainly upon the use of unfair tactics and not upon economies of large scale, he could

[13] F. H. Giddings, "The Persistence of Competition," *Political Science Quarterly*, II (1887), 65–66.

join laymen in calling for corrective legislation. Thus he did not have to accept the socialists' contention that the decline of competition was inevitable; and he was spared the embarrassment of arguing that the potential competition faced by a trust that totally controlled an industry was sufficient protection for the public interest.

Economists might differ in the importance that they attached to the part played by unfair competition in the rise of large firms (and by 1920 most had come to overestimate it). Yet by 1920 very few doubted that unfair competition had once existed, still did exist, or, in the absence of vigilance by the antitrust agencies, would exist again. So believing, economists gave their allegiance to the principle of an antitrust policy and, with the exception of a small, articulate minority, have never taken it back. There may be excellent reasons why economists of the 1960s should persist in this loyalty. The analysis of this chapter suggests, however, that continued fidelity ought to be founded on something more substantial than a belief that in a laissez-faire world there must be present a kind of competition that is, at once, both morally objectionable and economically wasteful.

In conclusion, we might note that the difficulty of demonstrating that economic warfare reduces social welfare creates a crisis of faith only for the professional economist. The layman's case for supporting laws intended to suppress unfair competition is simply that economic warfare is unfair. So long as he has no reason to believe that the cost of enforcing these laws is "excessive," the layman has no reason to withdraw his support.

CHAPTER 8 *Profit, Uncertainty, and Information*

1 · A VENERABLE AMBIGUITY. Throughout this book when we have referred to the theory of imperfect competition we have meant the theory of imperfect competition under conditions of perfect certainty. But of course, static theory is not enough. We have no wish to limit our study of imperfect competition in the real world to such features as can be explained with the aid of static theory. We also need economic models relevant to business behavior under conditions of uncertainty.

Until recently, relatively few economists have been self-conscious model builders. The older practice was rather to construct an implicitly static model and to append sensible remarks about how it differed from the real world. ("We shall assume that businessmen seek to maximize profits but of course, in reality, many prefer a quiet life to high profits gained at the cost of ulcers.") This *ad hoc* approach to uncertainty had the considerable merit of periodically reminding us of the limitations of static economic theory as an explanation of business behavior or as a guide to policy. Nevertheless, it has left us with a legacy of loose ends that is both aesthetically unsightly and wasteful of time and energy. We can set about liquidating, or at least reducing, this legacy by considering once more three venerable issues that appear when the uncertainty postulate is introduced: What is profit? Where does it come from? What role does it play in the decisions of businessmen?

In a static model these issues are virtually assumed away. When the model is static, in equilibrium, and perfectly competitive, all inputs earn the same rate of return and profit does not exist. When the model is static, in equilibrium, and imperfectly competitive, a component of income that is often mislabeled "monopoly profit" can exist but its explanation is self-evident. Moreover, in the second case, all inputs will appear (to the accountant) to earn the same rate of return, since the expected stream of "monopoly profits" will be capitalized into higher input prices. There being no uncertainty associated with production in a static model, the firm neither fears uncertainty nor requires a fund of liquid resources to cope with it. Hence the maximization of its income can plausibly be viewed as the firm's sole ambition.

Once uncertainty is introduced into the model, these simplicities dissolve. Now there is no expectation that profit will either be eliminated by movement toward equilibrium or disguised by capitalization. Nor is it now reasonable to assume that a businessman will have only one goal, or that different businessmen will all have the same mix of goals.

The problems of defining profit and identifying its origins can be disposed of quickly. With regard to the guidance function of profit, however, we shall have to accept a formidable dose of agnosticism. For our conclusion will be that no clearly defined role can be assigned to profit in business decision making. Indeed, we shall have to conclude that the scientific problem of explaining profit has very little in common with the scientific problem of explaining business motivation.

2 · MEASURES OF PROFIT. Over the years, economists and accountants have offered innumerable definitions of profit. We have not time or patience enough to consider many of them, but this is no great loss. While no single all-purpose definition of profit is possible, all the definitions that have gained wide favor with economists and accountants have been derived in essentially the same way and used for essentially the same end. Profit is always defined with reference to a specified accounting period; it is always equated with the difference between something called "revenue" and something called "cost"; and it is (almost) always used as an index of the "success" of an enterprise during the accounting period. The various influential definitions of profit differ in such relatively unimportant details as whether a bonus paid to a company executive at the end of the year should be reckoned as a part of profit or a part of cost. These definitions, however, differ also in the manner of allocating the costs of depreciation over successive accounting periods; and, though economists have shown little interest in the intricacies of depreciation accounting, the measurement of profit is largely a matter of allocating the costs of depreciation through time.

In the statistics on national income the term profit is used only in connection with the economic activities of firms that are organized as legal corporations. They contain an entry, *corporate profits before taxes,* and another, *corporate profits after taxes.* The taxes referred to in these entries are state and federal corporate income taxes; all other taxes borne by the corporation are treated as business expenses. For business and farm enterprises that do not take the corporate legal form, the national income statistics contain an entry, *net income of unincorporated enterprises,* which roughly corresponds to what economists and accountants regard as the "profits of small business."

Economists have many quibbles but few serious misgivings about the accounting rules used to derive the two corporate profit entries in the national income accounts. Both describe a residual that remains after the fixed and variable costs of operating an enterprise (mainly wages, salaries, rent, and interest on borrowed capital) have been met, including an allowance for the depreciation of plant and equipment used in production. This residual may be positive, negative, or zero. The economist does, however, have two reservations about the accountant's reckoning of corporate profit that ought to be noted. The first relates to the treatment of the return on so-called equity capital—that part of capital supplied by the legal owners of the corporation.

The economist contends that a more accurate picture of business success would result if, in reckoning profit, a deduction were made for implicit interest, that is, the return that equity capital could have earned if it had been invested outside the enterprise. Thus a corporation which over a period of years earns an average return of 3 per cent per annum on its equity capital is most probably an unsuccessful operation. With what most observers would view as average luck, the owners of the corporation could have secured a higher return with less risk by putting their investment stake into United States Government bonds.

The economist's second major reservation concerns the treatment of appreciation of the corporation's plant and equipment. He points out that it is illogical to write down the value of individual corporate assets as depreciation occurs while failing to write them up when appreciation occurs. (This is not to say that, in the valuation of assets, appreciation can be treated as the precise converse of depreciation.[1]) If asset depreciation is a cost, then asset appreciation is an addition to revenue and so ought to enter into the computation of profit. If pressed on the point, the economist will contend that the accounting distinction between profit and capital gain is largely without economic significance (though for reasons that we shall note presently, the distinction is not entirely without economic significance).[2]

3 · LADELLE ON PROFIT. In this connection we might note that, in 1890, the English accountant, O. G. Ladelle, proposed a revision of the accounting theory of profit that, if adopted, would have allayed most of the economist's misgivings about the treatment of capital gains and losses.[3]

[1] In the valuation of assets or, more accurately, in the reevaluation of assets, appreciation cannot be treated as the precise converse of depreciation because, unlike depreciation, it is almost always reckoned *ex-post;* that is, appreciation is almost always treated as a capital gain. One ordinarily expects that an individual capital asset will depreciate over time so that the actual depreciation of an asset as reckoned *ex-post* in the accounting period can be divided into that part which the purchaser anticipated when the asset was acquired (cost) and that part which he did not foresee (capital loss).

[2] The truth that no hard-and-fast distinction can be made between profit and capital asset appreciation was first brought home to economists by Frank Knight in the 1930s. See, for example, his introductory note to the 1940 reprint of *Risk, Uncertainty, and Profit* (No. 16 in the London School of Economics reprints of scarce tracts). The point had been made by a practicing accountant in a prize essay as early as 1890: O. G. Ladelle, "The Calculation of Depreciation," *The Accountant* (November 29–December 6, 1890).

[3] *Ibid.* The neglect of Ladelle is rather puzzling. Contributing factors were probably his early death shortly before his prize essay was published and the very cryptic statement of his thesis. The rediscovery of Ladelle was the work of Richard Brief, who had been trained in both economics and accounting. "A Late Nineteenth Century Contribution

Essentially Ladelle proposed that, when an asset is acquired, its depreciation be allocated *ex-ante* over the n accounting periods during which it is expected to remain in use. If in the ith accounting period the valuation of the asset were found to be more than original cost minus *ex-ante* depreciation, the capital gain discerned would be divided among the n accounting periods in proportion to the fraction of the total cost of *ex-ante* depreciation allocated to them. For example, if the *ex-ante* decision was that depreciation cost would be equal in all n periods, and a capital gain of $100 was discovered in the ith period, then a capital gain of $100/n$ would be assigned to each of the n periods.

Ladelle's proposal had the considerable merits of outlining an internally consistent way of treating capital gains and losses and underscoring the connection between profit and the divergence of *ex-post* results from *ex-ante* anticipations. To modernize Ladelle's proposed revision of profit theory it is necessary only to replace his point estimate of depreciation with a probability distribution. That is, we can direct that, when an asset is acquired, the purchaser construct a table of possible payoffs and assign a probability coefficient to each entry. If this rule were observed, the capital gains and losses subsequently realized by the firm would measure the success of its manager in predicting the future. The wholly successful

to the Theory of Depreciation," *Journal of Accounting Research,* V (Spring, 1967), 27–38. See also F. K. Wright, "An Evaluation of Ladelle's Theory of Depreciation," *Journal of Accounting Research,* V (Autumn, 1967).

It is also possible that Ladelle fell into neglect because he was going against the current in accounting theory which has made sound practice depend upon "objectivity" and "conservatism." He is clearly subjective in his insistence that the purchaser himself must set up a schedule of depreciation to reflect what he thinks will "really" happen and, by inference, adventurous as well in his treatment of capital gains and losses as arising from errors of managerial judgment.

manager would, of course, be one whose accounting records showed neither capital gains nor losses. And a capital gain would constitute the same indictment of managerial foresight as capital loss of equal amount.

4 · THE IMPOSSIBILITY OF MEASURING "TRUE" PROFIT. Unhappily, the economist's objections to the way in which accountants reckon corporate profit lead to the conclusion that there is no way in which "true" profit can be recorded. In order to secure the best approximation to the "true" profit of a firm it would be necessary to liquidate the firm under optimal circumstances. Thus one might closely approximate the profit earned by the General Motors Corporation since its inception by closing the company down over a fifty-year period and deducting all the costs incurred during its lifetime from all revenue (including capital gains) realized during its lifetime. Yet even liquidation under the most favorable circumstances is likely to yield an underestimate of the "true" profitability of a well-managed firm. The option to "keep going" is itself a thing of value; and complementarities among assets may be such that items which are useful as a part of a going concern may be nearly worthless once the sum of assets falls below some minimum threshold, for example, the underground transportation facilities of a bituminous coal mine.

The economist's criticisms of the treatment of corporate profit in the national income accounts apply, of course, with even greater force to their treatment of the income of unincorporated enterprises. For this category includes the income of farmers and small businessmen, much the greater part of which is clearly implicit payment for the labor services that they provide.

Still, the similarities between economic and accounting definitions of profit are, for our purposes, much more important than their differences. Both of them treat profit as a residual that is left when, during some accounting period (which can be as long or as short as one cares to make it), the total costs incurred by the firm are subtracted from its total revenue. The residual may be positive, negative, or zero; and it is widely regarded as an index of the "success" of the firm during the accounting period.[4]

5 · EXPECTED PROFIT AS A MANAGERIAL GOAL. When profit is equated with some surplus of revenue that remains to the owners of a firm after all costs of production are met, it is clear that we ought to be very careful about the role that we assign to profit in guiding production. One can view the real world as a simplistic econometric model where all business decisions in, say, the fiscal year 1968 are some function of the profits earned in different industries in fiscal 1967. Indeed, most teachers of economics have probably

[4] Not all writers minimize the differences between economists and accountants as regards the measurement of profit. See S. S. Alexander and David Solomons, "Income Measurement in a Dynamic Economy," in *Studies in Accounting Theory,* W. T. Baxter and Sidney Davidson, editors (Homewood, Ill., 1962), pp. 126–40.

The authors attach particular importance to the fact that "the economist regards income as the change in the recipient's entire command over goods and services over a given period" while "the accountant singles out certain transactions and confines his attention to the profit and loss on these transactions" (p. 133). This is true. So far as the *measurement* of profit is concerned, however, the difference does not seem to me to be significant. In an uncertain world it is simply not possible to measure a change in the recipient's entire command over goods and services—if only because the market values of some assets can only be estimated within limits. The economist, like the accountant, is reduced to measuring what can be measured.

adopted this expedient at one time or another in trying to explain the working of a capital market to particularly obtuse or sleepy sophomores. Nevertheless, there are two decisive objections to saying that future production is guided by past profit. The first is almost painfully obvious. To the extent that managers believe that past profit was due to circumstances that will not be present in the future, it does not influence their decisions relating to the future. The second objection is only slightly more sophisticated. The profit entry in the accounts of a firm is meaningless until it is related to the goals of its managers and to the risks that had to be run in order to seek them. (In the limiting case of the octogenarian millionaire who is running a small business to "keep occupied," a profit entry is wholly meaningless—running the business *is* the goal.)

Let us accept that business decisions for future years cannot be treated solely as a function of profit earned in past years. Can we not say simply: such decisions are guided by the prospect of profit in future years? This proposition is not "wrong." But it does contain more ambiguity than economists are comfortable with; and in their efforts to remove some of its ambiguity they have traveled three different roads.

The first road has led to the modern body of static economic theory, wherein the firm is made to operate with all production functions, factor prices, and demand functions given. On these assumptions, arbitrage in the factor and product markets "tends" to remove all differences in the rates of return on capital earned by different firms. When all such differences have disappeared, equilibrium has perforce been reached.

This approach to profit creates two methodological difficulties. The first we encountered in the guise of a terminological issue in Chapter 4. So long as competition is imperfect, arbitrage in the factor and product markets cannot eliminate all differences in rates of return on capital invested in different firms and different industries. It can only reduce them to some minimum which, moreover, may be unique to each firm or each industry. As we noted, it is purely a matter of verbal taste whether the permanent discrepancy between unit cost and price found in imperfect competition is called monopoly profit or an economic rent.

Monopoly profit can be got rid of by assuming away monopoly; and historically the effort to prove that, in static equilibrium, there is no profit has always involved the use of models of perfect competition. The construction of such a proof is beset with a number of pitfalls which need not concern us here.[5] Suffice it to say that economic models which exclude uncertainty have no value for illuminating the way in which real-world business decisions are influenced by the attitudes of businessmen toward uncertainty.

The second road traveled by economists in their efforts to clarify the role of profit in decision making has closely paralleled the first. It has led to what can be called static economic theory with multiple managerial goals. The premise that the firm has complete information on all matters relevant to all business decisions is retained. Now, however, the additional premise is introduced that profit maximization is not the only managerial goal. Thus one well-known view of business behavior assumes that, in the case of small business, the owner-manager seeks to maximize the utility of his income, such utility being a function of both profit earned and the number

[5] As all teachers of economic theory know, it is easy enough to prove that, given a linear, homogeneous, production function, in the equilibrium of perfect competition, "payments to the factors exhaust the product." The difficulties appear when the theorem is discussed in connection with other types of production functions. I have wrestled with these difficulties in *Modern Capital Theory* (New York, 1965), pp. 113–29.

of hours worked.[6] An equally well-known view assumes that, in the case of large firms, the goal is to maximize the growth of the firm subject to some profit constraint; that, for example, the managers will first seek to assure themselves of, say, a 10 per cent return on capital invested, and then maximize sales revenue.[7] (When the investment outlay that makes possible the growth of sales revenue is financed in part from retained earnings, this goal may, of course, involve the selection of a profit rate in excess of 10 per cent.) One author has even constructed a model where one of management's goals is "managerial slack"—a working environment wherein over-staffing makes for a more agreeable office life.[8] In principle, there is no limit, in addition to the desire for profits, to the number of managerial goals that may influence a firm's be-havior. Every economist must decide for himself whether the gain in realism that results from loading a static model with additional managerial goals is worth the loss of pedagogical clarity that results.

The third road traveled by economists in their effort to explain business behavior has required the painful discarding of certain assumptions of static economic theory. To this end, it is explicitly recognized that any business decision which has its payoff in the future involves risk and/or uncertainty. We shall presently question whether, in economic analysis, any meaningful distinction can be drawn between risk and un-certainty. The distinction is mentioned here because it is still made in widely used textbooks and treatises.

[6] T. Scitovsky, "A Note on Profit Maximization and Its Implications," *Review of Economic Studies,* XI (1943), 57–60.

[7] W. J. Baumol, "On the Theory of Expansion of the Firm," *American Economic Review,* LII (1962), 1078–87.

[8] O. E. Williamson, "A Model of Rational Managerial Behavior," *A Behavioral Theory of the Firm,* R. M. Cyert and J. G. March, editors (Englewood Cliffs, N.J., 1963), pp. 237–52.

6 · THE RISE OF PROFIT THEORY. While economists have always had something to say about the role of risk and/or uncertainty in economic life, the first systematic treatment of the subject can be taken as Frank Knight's *Risk, Uncertainty, and Profit* (1921). Although inconsistent in several important respects, Knight's classic is still worth a careful reading. It has been the point of departure for all subsequent work on profit, and it remains the patent source of the profit theory expounded in modern textbooks and treatises.

Knight on profit had the supreme heuristic merit of simplicity. The firm (entrepreneur) is presumed to hire factors "now" at known prices in order to make a product which will be sold "later" at an unknown price. Certain hazards of production were viewed by Knight as falling into the category of "risk"; thus, when a large number of enterprises are grouped together, it becomes economically feasible to organize an insurance program that protects the firm against such hazards. (The hazard of loss from fire is a traditional example of an insurable business risk.) For an insurance program to be economically feasible, two conditions must be satisfied: (a) there must exist a set of statistics that permits the organizers of the program to predict within narrow limits the aggregate business loss that will result from the hazards; and (b) the administrative costs of organizing the program must be low enough to attract enough participants to enable its organizers to take advantage of the Law of Large Numbers. When the hazards associated with production are of the type that can be insured against, insurance premiums become, according to Knight, costs of production akin to wages and raw material expenses. Profit, by definition, is what the firm has left after all the costs of production (implicit as well as explicit) have been met. Thus it is only those hazards which the firm cannot or will not insure against that constitute uncertainty. Only uncertainty can give rise to profit. As Knight was to emphasize in his later writings, profit can also take the form of an unforeseen appreciation in the value of the firm's inventory or capital equipment.

Not only does Knight, in *Risk, Uncertainty, and Profit,* trace the existence of profit to the fact of uncertainty in the business world. In his scheme, profit is payment for organizing production in the face of uncertainty. Hence, although profit may be a residual rather than a cost to a firm, from the larger standpoint of a capitalist economy, profit is clearly a cost. For, if it were not paid, entrepreneurs would not organize production in the face of uncertainty.[9]

7 · PROFIT THEORY AS A DEAD END. Over the years a number of serious criticisims have been directed at Knight's early views on profit.[10] The most telling was advanced

[9] In Knight's words: "The responsible decision relates to men rather than things; the ultimate manager is he who plans the organization, lays out functions, selects men for functions and appraises their value to the organization as a whole, in competition with all other bidders in the market. For this ultimate management there is but one possible remuneration, the residuum of product remaining after payment is made at rates established in competition with all owners for all services of men or things for which competition exists. This residuum is profit; it is the remainder out of the value realized from the sale of product after deduction of the values of factors in production which can be valued, or after all the product has been imputed to productive elements which can be imputed by the competitive mechanism. Profit is unimputable income, as distinguished from the total income of the owner of the business." *Risk, Uncertainty, and Profit* (Cambridge, 1921), p. 308.

[10] See, for example, J. F. Weston, "The Profit Concept and Theory: A Restatement," *Journal of Political Economy,* LXII (1954), 152–70; Martin Bronfenbrenner, "A Reformulation of Naive Profit Theory," *Southern Economic Journal,* XXVI (1960), 301–309; or H. B. Malm-

by Knight himself. In the introduction to the 1940 reprint of *Risk, Uncertainty, and Profit* he urged that its theory of profit needs to be "entirely reworked" in the light of the truth that all profit and loss arise through changes in the capital account. By his later argument, in a world of perfectly accurate book-keeping and an organized capital market, all profit and loss would arise through a change in the market value of a firm's assets. Moreover, the change in asset value would be registered at the moment that any change in expected future income was perceived by "the market." This instantaneous adjustment must occur because the value of the firm's assets is, by definition, equal to the sum of its discounted expected income (the rate of discount being the market rate of interest). The instantaneous capitalization of revised income expectations is, of course, closely approximated in the organized securities market since, as all sophisticated investors know, the ratio of a firm's annual income to the market value of its securities is largely meaningless as an index of its current success. A high ratio merely means that most investors believe that annual income will be less in the future. A low ratio merely means that most investors believe that it will be greater in the future.

There is a strong temptation to regard Knight's distinction between risk and uncertainty as interesting but obsolete. This temptation should be resisted, however, even though *Risk, Uncertainty, and Profit* contains no mention of the Reverend Thomas Bayes or subjective probability. The contradictions that caused Knight to recant his first theory of profit and prevent us from accepting his second have never been wholly resolved.

In retrospect on Knight, it is clear that the important variables in any decision made under conditions of uncertainty

gren, "Information, Expectations, and the Theory of the Firm," *Quarterly Journal of Economics,* LXXV (1961), 399–421.

are three: (a) the amount of information available to the decision maker; (b) his "degree of belief" in such information; and (c) his (subjective) estimate of the costs and benefits to be had from investment in the purchase or creation of more information. Here we can note that statisticians give the term risk a more specific meaning than did Knight; and that, by their definition, risk is not a phenomenon of the business world at all. By their usage, a risk situation is one wherein (a) every observer believes that he has all the obtainable information about a random variable; (b) every observer has complete confidence in his information; and (c) all observers act on the basis of the same information.

When these three conditions are present, the possibility that observers will invest in the creation or purchase of additional information simply does not arise. The true risk situation is epitomized by the well-mixed urn of the basic statistics course. When the urn contains an equal number of otherwise identical red and white balls, "everybody knows" that the probability that a blindfolded man will draw out a red ball is 0.5. No observer has any incentive to hire another as a consultant in estimating probabilities, and observers collectively have no incentive to establish a research program to learn more about red and white balls. In the business world, however, the decision maker never has complete information on the possible outcomes of an action or on their probabilities. His lot is uncertainty, not risk; and, by definition, "uncertainty involves future events about which there is incomplete knowledge or whose probability of occurrence is not 1." [11]

It follows, of course, that, when businessmen in "objectively similar" circumstances differ in their willingness to face uncertainty, have different amounts of information, and differ in

---

[11] J. F. Weston, "A Generalized Uncertainty Theory of Profits," *American Economic Review,* XL (1950), 43.

their degrees of belief in the information that they do have in common, they behave in different ways. It also follows that, in an uncertain world, it is entirely a matter of personal taste how one divides the payoff from a business decision into a return on capital invested, payment for uncertainty-bearing, and a capital gain. Thus the fact that a portfolio of blue chip common stocks carries a higher yield than a portfolio of United States Government bonds does not prove that *all* people who hold these stocks regard them as the more uncertain investment. It merely proves that *most* of the investors who can choose between the two believe that they are the more uncertain investment. Our willingness to speak of a "normal" or "prevailing" rate of return on capital merely reflects our belief that, most of the time, the majority of investors more accurately forecast investment outcomes than do the minority who venture to pit their judgment against the market.

On this assumption, a so-called "capital gain" is simply the investment payoff to which a "reasonable" investor, before the event occurred, assigned some very low probability coefficient. Therefore we must reject Knight's 1940 argument that profit is indistinguishable from capital appreciation.[12]

[12] Knight's later insistence on the identity of profit and the appreciation of capital assets is a good bad example of the tyranny of abstraction, that is, how one can misread reality after living too long with an economic model that one has constructed to illuminate reality. The identity between profit and capital asset appreciation would hold in a static model of perfect competition that is occasionally buffeted out of equilibrium by an Act of God which nobody believes that he can predict or cushion himself against. The Act, when it occurs, immediately restructures income expectations and so instantaneously gives rise to the capital gains and losses envisaged by Knight. It makes no difference whether a fortunate party collects his windfall immediately by selling his assets or more slowly through an increase in income spread over the accounting period.

In the real world the totally unforeseen event seldom occurs. The event which takes most people by surprise has usually been viewed as

Once we accept that, in objectively similar circumstances, different businessmen will behave differently when a decision involves uncertainty, the question whether businessmen seek to "maximize profit" acquires an Alice-in-Wonderland quality. Profit can only be measured *ex-post* by applying a uniform set of accounting conventions to raw figures. Yet the arbitrary character of these conventions (including the selection of the accounting period) ensures that the maximization of accounting profit cannot be the business goal. Unless one is prepared to accept some variety of accounting profit, for example, profit per annum or profit per decade, as a proxy for the unmeasurable true profit, to assert that businessmen seek to maximize profit is to assert that they seek to maximize something that cannot be measured.

8 · THE SEARCH FOR DECISION RULES. In recent years (especially since the appearance of *Theory of Games and Economic Behavior* in 1944) the interest of economists has shifted from the effort to identify what businessmen seek to maximize to the study of the so-called decision

a possibility by somebody before it happened. Hence, while a distinction between foresight and luck may be useful, it must necessarily be made in terms of some reasonable man criterion. The accounting profits or capital gains of a firm which strike corporate outsiders as due to luck may be viewed by corporate insiders as simply a "normal" return on their superior information.

Note also that Knight's notion of a "capital account," while it is precise enough when applied to a static model of perfect competition, becomes fuzzy when applied to the real world. For, given persisting uncertainty, the market value of a capital asset is known only within limits. Prior to the sale of the capital asset, one may estimate the possible prices that it will fetch and assign probability coefficients to them. But until the asset is actually sold—or income realized over time through its use—the profitability of owning it cannot be exactly known.

rules available to businessmen who must choose among alternatives under conditions of uncertainty. The new-style investigations have occasionally been naive in that writers have implied that a businessman "ought" to find a decision rule and stick to it.[13] But the discussion has been useful for illuminating business behavior when it has recognized that decision rules are merely abstractions from the "rules of thumb" or "short cuts" on which all business decisions in the real world are based.[14] And it is the fact that information has a cost that makes the use of rules of thumb "rational" and so provides the *raison d'être* for decision theory.

If the quantity of information available to the decision maker were fixed and immutable, there would be no problem. He would simply rank the alternative courses of action available to him according to their utility and choose the one at the top of the list. For example, suppose that the problem to be solved

[13] See, for example, M. K. Starr, "A Discussion of Some Normative Criteria for Decision-Making under Uncertainty," *Industrial Management Review,* VIII (Fall, 1966), 71–78.

[14] In the literature on industrial management, the term "decision rule" is sometimes given a narrower meaning than we have accepted for it in this chapter. On the assumption that the goals of the firm are given, it has been used as a synonym for "optimal solution" obtained when the firm maximizes some variable subject to constraints. For example, if the volume of output that the firm must produce in the next accounting period is given, and the relevant constraints are the cost of training new workers, the cost of securing additional output from the existing labor force at overtime rates of pay, and the cost of subcontracting output to other firms, the problem is simply to find the combination of new workers, overtime, and subcontracting that minimizes the total cost of the planned output. The solution of problems of this type may be tedious as far as computation is concerned, but in principle they are easily solved once the firm's production function and input costs are known. See C. C. Holt, Franco Modigliani, J. F. Muth, H. A. Simon, *Planning Production, Inventories, and Work Force* (Englewood Cliffs, N.J., 1960), especially Chapter 2, "Decision Rules for Planning Production and Work Force," pp. 47–63.

	Outcome	Probabil-ity	Expected Payoff	Minimum Gain
Bonds	7	1	7	7
	40	1/3		
Advertising	20	1/3	20	0
	0	1/3		
	90	1/3		
Machines	60	1/3	45	−15
	−15	1/3		

Table 8-1

is a simple one: invest $10,000 in the "best" way. Suppose further that no part of the $10,000 can be spent to secure more information about investment alternatives, and that the manager making the decision has three alternatives:

1. Invest $10,000 in United States Government bonds.
2. Invest $10,000 in machines.
3. Invest $10,000 in additional advertising.

In order to make a choice, the manager must assign a set of possible payoffs to each of the three alternative investments and a probability coefficient to each possible payoff. Let his estimates be given by the information in Table 8-1. The possible outcomes of each of the three investments are given as rates of return (in perpetuity). The subjective probability estimate of the manager that any outcome will occur is given by a corresponding rational fraction. For the reader's convenience, the minimum gain that the manager assigns to each investment alternative is also entered separately. Thus, if $10,-

000 is invested in advertising, the manager believes that three outcomes (expressed as rates of return) are possible; that they are 40, 20, and 0.0, respectively; and that all three outcomes are equally likely. The expected payoff from investment in advertising is 20, and the minimum gain is 0.0.

Since the information in Table 8-1 has, so to speak, been "revealed" to the manager by some agent in the universe and cannot be increased, he simply ranks the three alternatives according to their attractiveness (utility) and picks the top one. Any decision that he makes is economically rational in the all-important sense that "more is preferred to less." This is true because each of the three alternatives represents "more" by some reasonable criterion.[15] Thus investment in machines carries the highest (subjective) expectation of profit (45). Investment in bonds promises the greatest security as measured by the highest minimum gain (7). Investment in advertising is best for the judicious manager who will accept uncertainty provided that no part of his principal is endangered. In an uncertainty situation there would be a single best alternative only if one choice carried the greatest expected payoff *and* the least uncertainty as measured by every index of uncertainty that can be applied to the data.

It is true that decision rules are often—indeed, usually—discussed without reference to the costs of information. But this practice is unfortunate for two reasons. First, it fails to make clear to skeptics why decision rules are worth studying at all. For, as noted above, when all information on which a decision must be based is "given," the decision maker need

---

[15] For more rigorous observations on the problem of defining rational behavior under conditions of uncertainty, see A. G. Hart, *Anticipations, Uncertainty and Dynamic Planning* (New York, 1951), pp. 4–6; and Milton Friedman, *Price Theory: A Provisional Text* (Chicago, 1962), pp. 68–73.

only rank the alternatives according to their expected utility and select the most desirable one; that is, when all information is given, there is no need to employ a decision rule. Second, the failure to discuss decision rules in the context of a search for information means that the economically significant connection between the two goes unnoted. How much uncertainty the decision maker is prepared to accept depends partly upon the cost of securing information that may reduce it. Conversely, his demand for information depends partly upon his taste for uncertainty and so upon the decision rule chosen (every decision rule presupposing that a certain amount of information has already been gained).

When a decision rule is used, the presumption must be that the decision maker believes that it equates the marginal cost and expected marginal value of information. But businessmen differ in the "degrees of belief" that they place in any given amount of information, in the degrees of belief that they have in the opinions of outside consultants, and in their willingness to bear uncertainty. Hence every industry is populated by businessmen who operate according to different decision rules (rules of thumb), and transfer their allegiance from one rule to another with great frequency.

Here we might digress to emphasize a truth well known to Bayesian statisticians: the value of a decision rule to a manager can never be inferred from the outcome of the decision itself except insofar as the execution of the decision generates information relevant to future decisions. This is the case whenever business decisions are repetitive, for example, when a trucking firm with a large fleet must decide whether to replace engines after 80,000, 100,000, or 120,000 miles. The firm can try all three options and compare the results. The execution of a decision rule can also create useful information in the "A" or "not A" case. Suppose that an inexperienced grain elevator operator decides to hedge his inventory against a fall in the price of wheat for six months. Then, at the end of this trial period, he will have acquired information that allows him to compute what he could have gained by not hedging.

But many once-in-a-lifetime decisions are so unique that their execution adds virtually nothing to the manager's stock of useful information about alternatives. Should a port city decide to develop a stretch of the waterfront for shipping uses in preference to other alternatives, it may well be impossible in future years to tell whether the decision rule employed by the city fathers was optimal. For in electing to develop for shipping uses, they gave up their option to secure information on what the waterfront stretch would have earned if developed as an industrial park or residential complex.

9 · RECAPITULATION. Earlier generations of economists whose thinking was still closely constrained by definitions and linguistic usages taken over from the business world mostly accepted that businessmen seek to maximize something called profit. They viewed the task of clarifying business motivation as one of distilling "pure," "economic," or "true" profit from the raw material of accounting data. Although this search had some valuable intellectual by-products (it certainly helped to clarify the concept of economic uncertainty), it was ultimately unsuccessful. It led to the conclusions that: (a) profit (other than "monopoly profit"), however defined, exists only in an uncertain world; and, (b) since different businessmen have different attitudes toward uncertainty, they obviously do not seek to maximize anything that can be identified as profit in the national income accounts. Nor do they seek to maximize their subjective mathematical expectations of profit. One dis-

tinguished economist has even attempted to expunge the term "profit" from his professional vocabulary.[16]

As the realization grew that further revisions of profit theory could not throw further light on business motivation, the problem was rephrased to read: assuming the existence of uncertainty, what rule will a businessman who, *ceteris paribus,* prefers more of a good thing to less of a good thing use to choose among alternatives. Rephrasing of the question led, in turn, to realization that the difficult problem in explaining business behavior is not to distinguish between rational and irrational choices when alternatives exist. Rather it is to explain how businessmen go about identifying alternatives in the first place. This brings us down to the present. That a businessman when faced with uncertainty may choose to invest in a search for information that may reduce uncertainty is clear enough. The study of decision rules which can (or actually do) guide his search for information is just beginning.

[16] Milton Friedman prefers to speak of "non-contractual costs"—the difference between total receipts and total contractual costs. This residuum can, in turn, be subdivided into the expected part ("rent" or "quasi-rent") and the unexpected part ("pure profit"). But, here again, the question is: expected by whom? *Price Theory,* pp. 98–99.

CHAPTER 9 *Economic Activity as Learning*

1 · COMPETITION AND INFORMATION. The first five chapters of this book presented a restatement of the theory of imperfect competition under static conditions. Chapters 6, 7, and 8 then examined some of the results which follow when the assumptions needed for static equilibrium are relaxed. Now the time has come to deal more explicitly with an issue that has repeatedly intruded in our discussions—the role of information in competition. Specifically, let us set about resolving a paradox propounded earlier. Economists assume that perfect competition requires complete information about all current and future transactions in the market; yet we have seen that complete information will also cause all plants in an industry to be placed under unified central management. We shall postpone, until later in this chapter, an examination of the problems that arise when we seek to define and measure "information."

We are not without clues as to how the paradox of information and competition can be resolved. One has been provided by G. J. Stigler's observation that a major source of confusion in economic theory has been the failure to distinguish perfect competition from a perfect market.[1] Another has been afforded

[1] *Essays in the History of Economics* (Chicago, 1965), pp. 244–45.

by J. M. Clark's demonstration that the preoccupation of economists with economic equilibrium has caused them to lose sight of much that is important in the competitive process.[2] It is possible for us to be more precise. The most important factor overlooked in this preoccupation is the role of information in competition. Let us begin our effort to remedy this neglect by considering the part played by information in the classic duopoly problem of economic theory. Duopoly is, after all, the simplest form of competitive, that is, non-collusive market structure and, hence, the proper place to begin.

2 · DUOPOLY WITH (VIRTUALLY) NO INITIAL INFORMATION. All the well-known solutions (those of Cournot, Bertrand, Edgeworth) of the duopoly problem are based upon assumptions that limit the amount of information that each firm can accumulate. Indeed, such a limit is absolutely necessary in order to keep duopoly from being transformed into monopoly. For once the duopolists, acting alone or together, assemble enough information to calculate the demand for their industry's product and predict each other's response to price or output changes, they will either cooperate to maximize joint profits or one will buy out the other.

For our purposes the most relevant formulation of the duopoly problem is that which throws most light on competition as a learning process. This is the "black box" case of duopoly whose properties seem to have been investigated first by W. S. Vickrey. (In formal information theory the black box

[2] *Competition as a Dynamic Process* (Washington, 1961), especially pp. 54–56.

is the "machine" about which nothing is known except the past association of certain inputs with certain outputs.[3])

Assume:

1. Two different firms simultaneously come into possession of mineral springs.
2. There is no cost of producing or marketing mineral water.
3. Each spring can produce a finite amount of mineral water, but the combined maximum outputs of the two springs at least suffice to provide the quantity demanded at a zero price.

These assumptions are, of course, taken directly from Cournot and Betrand. But here we part company with them by assuming in addition:

4. The two owners know only that a demand for mineral water may exist; they do not know what it is.
5. The two owners are, initially at least, totally unaware of each other's existence.
6. Both owners have had a training in the "classical" theory of probability.
7. Three exists (unknown to the duopolists) a linear demand curve for mineral water which is constant over time.

The problem that we wish to solve is: given the above assumptions, what equilibrium output, if any, will emerge? Specifically, will the duopolists be able to learn enough about the industry demand curve and each other's behavior to reach

[3] An excellent introduction to the black box view of the world is given by W. R. Ashby, *An Introduction to Cybernetics* (New York, 1957), pp. 86–117.

monopoly equilibrium? W. S. Vickrey has surmised that, on the above assumptions, the duopolists will not be able to gain the information needed to achieve this state. Instead, he has reckoned that the process of learning by doing will lead them finally to settle into a Cournot equilibrium where output (given a linear demand curve and zero production cost) is two-thirds of the total quantity demanded at a zero price.[4]

3 · VICKREY'S SOLUTION. On close inspection it appears that Vickrey's solution to the duopoly problem with (virtually) complete ignorance is clearly correct if two further assumptions are introduced:

8. The duopolists have (virtually) no memory; that is, each one determines whether a change in his output has made him better off or worse off by comparing his present state with his previous state only.
9. The duopolists seek information by varying output by small increments, for example, by producing outputs of n, $n + 1$, and $n - 1$.

The formal proof of Vickrey's theorem is rather tedious (since each firm's behavior must be carried through a large number of moves). For our purposes it will suffice to show that, if, by chance, the duopolists reach Cournot equilibrium on the first "play," then the information secured by incrementally random behavior on a subsequent play will not upset this equilibrium. That is, each duopolist will independently conclude that his output in Cournot equilibrium is more profitable "on average" than either a slightly smaller or slightly larger output.

[4] W. S. Vickrey, *Microstatics* (New York, 1964), pp. 305–08.

Whenever a firm begins production with incomplete information about its demand function, it will, for a time at least, go through a "search phase" in which it deliberately varies output in order to obtain additional information. Indeed, the firm will not entirely abandon such exploratory behavior until it has concluded that the value of the additional information obtainable through further search is less than the income sacrificed by using output variation as a search tool. There are, of course, innumerable search strategies that each duopolist could adopt. And he will never be in a position to identify the best one until he has gained complete information. Yet, as we shall see presently, the search is likely to be called off before this state is reached. Hence neither duopolist has any reason to believe that his strategy is optimal except in the limited sense that, after it has, for a time, been used to generate information, a shift to a different strategy would cost "too much." (In this respect the information secured by the adoption of a particular search strategy is merely one more fixed cost of production.) Since innumerable search strategies are possible and search usually ceases before the best one has been discovered, we must arbitrarily specify the search strategy that our duopolists will follow.[5]

[5] Some information theorists prefer to divide the learning process into "search" and "hill climbing." Search is equated with an initial phase where performance does not rise essentially above its initial level, and hill climbing with the later phase "wherein the machine improves its marginal success as far as possible." If this distinction is accepted, the incrementally random behavior of our duopolists as described above becomes hill climbing.

When the object is to gain altitude, hill climbing has the advantage of carrying one to a peak in a reasonably efficient manner. But if the terrain contains more than one peak, there is no assurance that it will carry one to the highest peak. On these matters see Marvin Minsky and O. G. Selfridge, "Learning in Random Nets," in *Information Theory*, Colin Cherry, editor (London, 1961), pp. 335–47.

Let the "true" demand curve for mineral water be given by some linear function where P denotes output and Q quantity demand, say,

$$P = 120 - Q \qquad (1)$$

Let each "play" consist of 1000 consecutive "moves" made according to a predetermined strategy. Finally, let each duopolist, as a part of the random behavior of his search strategy, elect to produce 40 units on each of the 1000 moves that constitute the first play. Thus total output for the industry is 80 units per move and price per unit is $40. Assuming that complete records are kept, each duopolist will know that he gained a profit of $1600 on every move of the first play.

During the 1000 moves of the second play let the two producers seek additional information about demand by choosing their output at random from the set 39, 40, 41 and record the payoff after every move. If at the end of the second play each duopolist fits a regression line to the data generated by the 1000 moves of this play, he will find that it approximates

$$P = 80 - Q \qquad (2)$$

The value of the constant term (80) in equation (2) is obtained by subtracting the expected value of the rival duopolist's output (40) during the second play from the value of the constant term (120) in equation (1).

Independently of each other, our duopolists will draw the following two inferences. First, during the 1000 moves of the second play, the mean payoff of an output of 40 units was greater than that of either 39 or 41 units. Second, the regular output of 40 units during the first play yielded a greater aggregate payoff than the fluctuating (39, 40, 41) output of the second play. Hence on the third and all subsequent plays each duopolist will produce 40 units on every move. Equilibrium has been reached, and it is the same as Cournot's.

4 · ALTERNATIVES TO VICKREY'S SOLUTION. There is, however, no certainty that the Cournot equilibrium deduced by Vickrey for black box duopoly will be reached if the players have a memory that extends back beyond the two most recent plays. Suppose, for instance, that during the 1000 moves of the first play each duopolist on every move produces 30 units and so gains a payoff of $1800. Suppose, that is, that the duopolists begin the game by producing the aggregate output that maximizes their joint profits but have no knowledge of their good fortune.

On each of the 1000 moves of the second play, let both duopolists seek additional information by choosing output at random from the set, 29, 30, 31. When the data generated by the output variations of the second play have been recorded, each player will face a dilemma.

On the one hand, he perceives that average payoff per move was less during the second play than during the first play. For the output that maximized joint profits (60 units) was produced on every move of the first play, but on only about one move in three of the second play. On the other hand, each duopolist notes that, on the (approximately) 333 moves of the second play when he produced 31 units, average payoff was (approximately) $1829 and hence greater than the $1800 payoff per move on the first play.

A pair of timid players, beginning with the third play, will abandon the search for more information and return to the steady output of 30 units, which they produced during the first play. A somewhat more adventuresome pair can be imagined as seeking additional information during the third play by selecting output at random from the set 30, 31, 32. For each player the approximate payoff per move will be $1720 for 30 units, $1798 for 31 units, and $1824 for 32 units. But each player will recall that during the second play, outputs of 31 units yielded the higher average payoff of (approximately) $1829. Hence the duopolists will independently conclude that the search for additional information is unprofitable and, beginning with the fourth play, will return to the steady output of 30 units per move.

In the above black box example we have allowed the duopolists to accidentally stumble into the monopoly equilibrium that maximizes their joint profits. Is there any discernible search strategy for a duopolist that can ensure this outcome? The answer must be no unless we introduce the additional assumptions that (a) the black box contains a method of communication by which the duopolists can exchange information with each other and (b) both duopolists possess the skills needed to discover and make use of the method. Thus, if the black box duopoly game were being played on a computer by two veteran gamesmen from the Carnegie-Mellon University, one would expect that, in very short order, communication would be established, information exchanged, and monopoly equilibrium reached. If the game were being played by a Japanese importer and an Afghan rug merchant, such an outcome would be, to put it mildly, most unlikely. In any event, in black box duopoly the actions of one player ensure that the other player can never gather, by his own unaided efforts, the information that will allow him to deduce the "true" demand curve for the industry's product.

Actually the problem of locating stable equilibrium in black box duopoly is very similar to that of the conventional cases where the producers are presumed to have perfect knowledge of the industry's demand curve but imperfect knowledge of the rival's behavior. In both situations, each must be presumed to have strategy that combines the use of existing information with the search for additional information. In both situations the strategy that is selected by one duopolist necessarily influences the information that is generated by the corresponding strategy of the other.

5 · TWO POLICY ISSUES REVISITED. The discussion of black box duopoly presented above has some intriguing implications for public policy toward industrial organization though, here again, one must tread warily. Let us consider two long-debated questions in the light of what we have learned. What will be the consequences for price and output of increasing the number of firms in a black box market? What will be the consequences for price and output of reducing the amount of uncertainty in a black box market?

In the example used above we have followed Cournot by positing that entry into the industry is closed; therefore any profits earned by the original duopolists cannot result in additional mineral springs being brought into production. Given this premise, an increase in the number of firms in a black box market cannot raise equilibrium price. For the addition of another firm does not, by itself, permit producers to form a more accurate estimate of industry demand or to gain additional information about one another's behavior. However, an increase in the number of firms in a black box market may bring about a lower equilibrium price. Indeed, given (virtually) no memory and variations in output that are incremental and random, an increase in numbers must lower equilibrium price in precisely the same way as in Cournot's original analysis.[6] Thus, when

[6] Vickrey, *Microstatics,* pp. 307–08.

the industry demand curve is linear (and production cost is zero), equilibrium output Q_e is given by

$$Q_e = \frac{n}{n+1} Q_0$$

where n is the number of firms and Q_0 is the output which will be demanded at a zero price.

But let us be clear that, could we, by waving a wand, transform a black box market into one wherein all producers have complete information about industry demand, the question of entrepreneurial numbers would become irrelevant. The industry promptly moves to the monopoly price that maximizes joint profits; nor can this result be blocked by introducing antitrust rules that forbid mergers and cartels. Firms would still have the alternative of using information about demand to institute a follow-the-leader (any leader) behavior that would lead them to monopoly equilibrium.[7] Therefore, in an industry in which the entry of new firms is impossible, the application of antitrust rules which seek to perpetuate ignorance (e.g., by denying firms the right to exchange information among themselves on past transactions or future production plans) has much to recommend it. This proposition applies also to antitrust rules designed to create or preserve some minimum number of firms in the no-entry industry.

However, should our example be revised to allow for the possibility that new mineral springs can be brought into production but at a cost, these two presumptions in favor of antitrust rules must be discarded. In black box duopoly where the existing firms can supply the entire quantity demanded at a

[7] For some possible paths by which a monopoly equilibrium is reached when oligopolists cannot directly communicate with each other, see R. L. Bishop, "Duopoly: Collusion or Warfare?," *American Economic Review*, L (1960), 931–61.

zero price, it is clear that no resources ought to be used to bring additional mineral springs into production. Yet, if incomplete or inaccurate information about the industry is circulating among prospective investors, a newcomer may decide to gamble on the development of another spring. The danger of such wasteful investment disappears as soon as firms in the industry have gained complete information and use it to place their plants under a unified central management that practices stay-out pricing. Should this be done, we once more have the proximate output of perfect competition with the misleading facade of monopoly.

In the late nineteenth century, defenders of the emerging trusts justified them on the ground, *inter alia,* that they eliminated the wastes of competition represented by the financial and human losses resulting from frequent bankruptcies and other business failures. Economists have always been quick to challenge this argument, though not always for the same reasons. Many once rejected it for no better reason than that it served the private interests of the trust organizers. But clearly the argument has always contained some portion of truth. Insofar as competition defined as a multiplicity of rival firms exists because uncertainty exists, the so-called "wastes of competition" are merely the private and social costs of organizing production in the face of uncertainty. They can be expected to disappear as the elimination of uncertainty destroys the raison d'être of competition so defined.

6 · COMPETITION AND INFORMATION THEORY. Our discussion of black box duopoly also serves to throw light on the venerable, if imprecisely formulated, issue: Does competition contain some inherent tendency to "break down"? If by competition is meant the exploratory behavior of a firm

economists implies no measure or index of information (or uncertainty).

In formal information theory, information is a quantitative, operational concept, although even here it has not yet acquired a single, unambiguous connotation.[11] However, in the great majority of cases it refers to one of three magnitudes: (a) the amount of uncertainty expressed in "bits" that the transmission of a message has removed; (b) the amount of uncertainty expressed in bits that *a priori* the observer expects that the transmission of a message to remove; or (c) the accumulation of data that reduce the amount of uncertainty attaching to future decisions (this amount again being measured in bits) that the observer faces as he moves through states S_1, S_2, . . ., S_n. It is this last meaning that is most relevant to economic analysis.

Consider the most frequently used example in information theory. A coin is to be tossed and a message transmitted that states the outcome of the toss. Before the event there are two possible outcomes and two (equal) prior probabilities. Should the message transmitted state that the outcome of the toss is a head, then one alternative has been eliminated. In information theory the message which, when transmitted, eliminates one of two equally likely possibilities is said to contain one "bit" of information. Alternatively, it is said to eliminate "one bit of variety" (bit being the contraction of binary digit). Indeed, in formal information theory, all the significant quantities— variety, information transmitted, entropy, and information gain —are usually expressed as so many "bits."

In the coin-tossing case two outcomes are possible; and, since $\log_2 2 = 1$, it has become the practice to use logarithms to the base 2 in reckoning the number of bits. Thus the state-

---

[11] On definitions of "information" see D. K. MacDonald, "Information Theory and Its Application to Taxonomy," *Journal of Applied Physics,* XXIII (1952), 529–31.

ment that "an event whose prior probability was P has, in fact, occurred" is denoted by

$$I(P_i) = \log_2 \frac{1}{P_i} \tag{3}$$

or

$$I(P_i) = -\log_2 P_i \tag{3a}$$

Note that, the smaller the value of P, the greater is the amount of uncertainty removed by receipt of the message.

7 · INFORMATION GAIN. For our purposes the important idea in information theory is that of *expected* information gain. Whenever more than one outcome is possible, every message transmits information—it records an outcome. But not every message transmits information that will cause the recipient to alter his behavior in the future. To a gambler the probability that a coin in a fair toss will fall heads is, of course, 0.5. His discovery that the outcome of a particular toss was heads will not cause him to change his betting habits. For him, receipt of the message has not brought an expected information gain. There is such a gain only when the message transmitted allows the recipient to compute a new set of probabilities that make the amount of uncertainty in the present state less than the amount in the previous state.

It follows that, to the extent that the player gains information through a series of plays, the amount of information that can be transmitted by the message recording the outcome of the next play is correspondingly reduced. In the limiting case wherein the player has gained enough information to allow him to assign a probability coefficient of 1.0 to a single outcome (i.e., in the case in which he has acquired what we loosely call "complete information") a message that confirms his prediction perforce carries no information.

Let $P = (p_1, p_2, \ldots, p_n)$ denote the set of prior probabilities that exists before the transmission of the message, and $Q = (q_1, q_2, \ldots, q_n)$, the set of prior probabilities that exists after its receipt and before the transmission of a second message. In the black box duopoly example of this chapter, P could represent the set of probabilities computed from sales data accumulated during the first play, and Q the set of probabilities computed from sales data accumulated during the second play.

The uncertainty existing before transmission of the first message is given by

$$H(P) = -\sum_{i=1}^{m} p_i \log_2 p_i \qquad (4)$$

The uncertainty existing after receipt of the first message and before the transmission of the second message is given by

$$H(Q) = -\sum_{i=1}^{n} q_i \log_2 q_i \qquad (5)$$

We can also describe $H(P)$ as the expected information content of the first message and $H(Q)$ as the expected information content of the second message. Note that $H(P)$ and $H(Q)$ always take positive values. For since $0 < p_i < 1$ and $0 < q_i < 1$, $\log_2 p_i < 0$ and $\log_2 q_i < 0$. The expected information gain $I(G)$ resulting from the transmission of the first message is therefore

$$I(G) = H(P) - H(Q) \qquad (6)$$

Expected information loss is also a logical possibility and occurs whenever

$$H(Q) > H(P)$$

That is, expected information loss occurs whenever the observer concludes, after receipt of a message, that "something in the black box" has increased the amount of uncertainty that he must face on his next play.[12]

Finally, we observe that in equations (4) and (5) the expected information content of the message H is greatest when the prior probabilities of the outcomes are equal. This property is easily verified by reverting to natural logarithms and maximizing the expression [13]

$$-\sum_{i=1}^{k} x_i \log_e x_i \quad \text{subject to the constraint} \quad \sum_{i=1}^{k} x_i = 1$$

In our example of black box duopoly, each producer, after the first play of the contest, was viewed as basing his strategy upon the statistics generated by one or more of the preceding plays. We assumed that he would use the data to compute a statistical demand curve. Given this behavior, each duopolist will continue to search for additional information, by varying output, as long as the information gain generated by this exploratory behavior serves to increase the net worth of the

---

[12] What we have defined above as the expected information gain $I(G)$ corresponds closely, but not exactly, to what Henri Theil has called "the reduction of information caused by the message." In his notation this reduction is $I(q:p)$. Theil also holds that "$I(q:p)$ can also be regarded as the reduction of uncertainty caused by the message which is evidently a natural measure for the value of the message." *Applied Economic Forecasting* (Chicago, 1966), pp. 260–61.

[13] Use the Lagrangian form

$$-\sum_{i=1}^{k} x_i \log_e x_i - \lambda \left(\sum_{i=1}^{k} x_i - 1 \right)$$

We differentiate with respect to x_i and λ and put the result equal to zero. Then $\log_e x = -1 - \lambda$ for every i. Hence the prior probabilities where H is a maximum are all equal to k^{-1}.

enterprise (which, in the case where cost of production is zero, is simply the sum of discounted expected future revenues).

Let us be clear that, in black box duopoly, equilibrium cannot be defined as the state where both producers believe that they have complete information on the market simply because $H(P) = H(Q) = 0$. Nor can equilibrium here be defined as the state where both producers believe that, although complete information is not possible, no information gain is possible from further search because $H(P) = H(Q) = K > 0$. Once the firm has acquired some information about the market, the resort to exploratory behavior to secure further information imposes some sacrifice of income. Information has a cost. This being so, the firm will discontinue the search phase of its operation before all the uncertainty (entropy) that can be eliminated by exploratory behavior has, in fact, been eliminated.[14] And, in any economic system, the exploratory behavior of firms that is one feature of the competitive process will finally cease, or become economically insignificant, unless one or both of two developments take place. The observer reaches the limit of his capacity to store data because, at some point, he begins to "forget" or because the cost of storing data of little economic value becomes "prohibitive"; or the predicative value of the data in the observer's possession is constantly being destroyed by exogenous forces.

[14] The problems of search theory, especially as they arise from the possibility of using price or output variations to secure information, have received little systematic attention in economics. See, however, J. E. Haring and G. C. Smith, "Utility Theory, Decision Theory, and Profit Maximization," *American Economic Review,* XLIX (1959), 566–83. For the origins of search theory see the pioneer papers of B. O. Koopman, "The Optimum Distribution of Effort," *Operations Research,* I (1953), 52–63, and "The Theory of Search, III. The Optimum Distribution of Searching Effort," *Operations Research,* V (1957), 613–26; and G. J. Stigler, "The Economics of Information," *Journal of Political Economy,* LXIX (1961), 213–25.

A second truth is of nearly equal importance. The co-existence of two or more producers of the same product, which is also a feature of the competitive process, will give way to the rationalization that produces a unified central management unless the same processes of data destruction and obsolescence are at work.[15] As we have emphasized on prior occasions in this book, the elimination of firms that occurs as the uncertainty surrounding production diminishes ought never to be equated with "monopoly."

In the real world a formidable array of forces is always at work to destroy data or reduce their economic value. Men learn, but their knowledge is lost through death, forgetting, or inability to communicate with the young. Consumer tastes change inexplicably, new products and new production techniques appear. Nevertheless, it would seem to be a valid gen-

---

[15] In his article on the relevance of information theory to economic theory, Professor R. A. Jenner accepts that the reduction of uncertainty tends to produce monopoly. Nevertheless, he argues that competition does not break down because, as the monopolist comes to dominate the market, the absence of competitors removes him from "active experimentation with new ideas" and "a gap will grow between those products consumers in fact 'choose' on the monopolized market and what they would choose if they were given the opportunity, that is, if the market were perfectly competitive." This is essentially the argument of Alfred Marshall and many older economists that monopolists "go soft."

This argument may be correct; and it can probably be fashioned into a hypothesis that can be tested empirically. But there is nothing in the sole possession of a market that necessarily causes the established firm to abandon the information search that represents active experimentation with new ideas. Indeed, given the persistence of uncertainty, the established firm will never completely abandon the search effort. The most one can say is that, the more rapidly exogenous forces alter the business environment, the greater is the likelihood that the established firm will guess wrong and yield part of its market to newcomers in any finite span of time. See R. A. Jenner, "An Information Version of Pure Competition," *Economic Journal*, LXXVI (1966), 786–805.

eralization that, in the absence of antitrust rules, there is a universal tendency for "industries" to be brought under unified central management with the passing of time. In the few sectors of the American economy where concentration ratios have fallen over time without the application of trust busting, the gain in competition has probably been more apparent than real. It can generally be traced to the tyranny of words, and most commonly to the failure to recognize that the character of the "product" produced by the "industry" has radically changed between two dates. Competition viewed either as a search for information or the persistence of a multiplicity of producers seems to require the unsettling flow of new products.

8 · RECAPITULATION. As long as a firm is uncertain about the demand for its industry's product or the behavior of rival firms or, for that matter, about the effect of alternative outputs on its own cost of production, it will use variations in output or price as a method of securing information. As information is generated and put to use, the fraction of "moves" devoted to search effort will be reduced. Rival firms will further reduce uncertainty by pooling information. And the industry via a merger or cartel will acquire the look of monopoly. At the same time the rationalized, single enterprise will begin to produce, at a stable rate, the minimum output necessary to dissuade other firms from entering the industry. If the gain in information as production continues through time is not to reduce both the number of exploratory price or output changes and the number of firms, it must be offset by events that, by destroying data or undermining their predictive value, maintain the existing amount of uncertainty.

Appendix · A NOTE ON LEARNING AND THE DECLINE
OF COMPETITION

Problem

Since the connections among learning, the level of information,
and the decline of competition form a subject often mentioned
but seldom systematically explored in economic theory, there may
be merit in considering them in some detail. We shall limit our
exploration to the case of duopoly where production is associated
with uncertainty and the industry is completely closed to additional producers. Our problem is to identify the conditions that
must be satisfied before one duopolist will sell out to the other,
when, beginning in a state of incomplete information, each
"learns" with the passing of time.

Assumptions

(a.1) Production is carried through time periods $t = 1, 2, \ldots, n,$
where n takes a value greater than any assigned real number.

(a.2) When $t = 1$, each firm has more information about its own
operation than about that of the rival.

(a.3) As $t \to \infty$, the amount of A's information about his own
operation and the amount of A's information about B's
operation tend to the same limit.

(a.4) The market situations and learning patterns of the duopolists, A and B, are replicates; so that any statement that is
true for A becomes, after the appropriate change in notation, true for B.

(a.5)
$$V_A^t(A) = \alpha[I_A^t(A) + I_A^t(B)] \tag{1}$$

shall be read: The value that A, at time t, places upon his
own operation is equal to a constant multiplied by the sum

of A's information about his own operation and A's information about B's operation.

(a.6) $V_A^t (A \cup B) = \beta[I_A^t(A)\, I_A^t(B)]$ (2)

shall be read: The value that A places upon the industry *operated as a rationalized monopoly* is equal to a constant multiplied by the product of A's information about his own operation and A's information about B's operation.[16]

Inferences

By (a.2) and (a.3), A's information about his own operation at time t can be written

$$I_A^t(A) = \frac{K}{e^{\lambda/t}}$$ (3)

and A's information about B's operation at time t can be written

$$I_A^t(B) = \frac{K}{e^{2\lambda/t}}$$ (4)

In the language of game theorists, the rivalry of A and B will be transformed from a non-cooperative game into a cooperative game if and when A and B independently conclude that the industry is worth more as a single rationalized enterprise than as two imperfectly coordinated firms. In layman's language, if and when this condition is fulfilled, competition will "break down." The merging of A and B requires that

$$V_A^t(A \cup B) - V_A^t(A) \geq V_B^t(B)$$ (5)

Since, by (a.4), $V_A^t(A) = V_B^t(B)$, equation (5) can be written

$$V_A^t(A \cup B) \geq 2V_A^t(A)$$ (5a)

---

[16] Thus $I_A^t(A)$ in the above notation corresponds to G. B. Richardson's "primary information," and $I_A^t(B)$ to his "secondary information." "Equilibrium, Expectations, and Information," *Economic Journal*, LXIX (1959), 223–37.

Substituting from (3) and (4) in (5a) and simplifying, we have

$$\frac{\beta K}{2\alpha} \geq e^{\lambda/t} + e^{2\lambda/t} \tag{5b}$$

To find $t,^*$ the minimum positive value for t that satisfies equation 5b), we let $C = e^{\lambda/t}$, $h = \beta k/2\alpha$, and write

$$h = C + C^2 \tag{6}$$

We can rewrite equation (6) in quadratic form and solve directly for the two values of C. Discarding the negative root as being without economic meaning, we have

$$C = (h + \tfrac{1}{4})^{\frac{1}{2}} - \tfrac{1}{2} \tag{7}$$

Since $e^{t/\lambda} = C$,

$$t^* = \log_e \left[(h + \tfrac{1}{4})^{\frac{1}{2}} - \tfrac{1}{2}\right]\lambda \tag{8}$$

Note that, when $0 < t^* \leq 1$, the industry will never be competitive. The game begins at $t = 1$, and the duopolists already have enough information to perceive the folly of rivalry. They will combine "immediately."

Note also that there may be no positive value for t that satisfies equation (5b). That is, at no time will they combine.

In (5b),

$$\lim_{t \to \infty} (e^{\lambda/t} + e^{2\lambda/t}) = 2$$

To stipulate $\beta k/2\alpha \geq 2$ is to ensure that the duopolists can never gain enough information to conclude that cooperation is worthwhile.

Reflections

We have considered the duopoly case where rival firms begin production with incomplete information, do not fear the entry of new firms, and learn by doing. We have assumed that the passing of time serves to disseminate information by increasingly making A's information known to B and B's information known to A. And we have concluded that, in such a case, learning is a force working toward monopoly; and that, unless a low limit is placed upon the amount of information that both firms can acquire, learning must necessarily produce monopoly at some point in time.

The preceding analysis could easily be adapted to cover the case of an industry initially consisting of three or more firms. With considerably more difficulty it could be broadened to cover the case where the entry of additional firms is a possibility. The important truth, however, is that competition defined as a state consisting of two or more firms is undermined by the learning process. For competition so defined to persist, there must be a limit to the amount of information—information again being defined as that which reduces uncertainty—that each firm can acquire. The limit may be imposed by the limitations of the learner or the intrusion of exogenous forces that create for him new uncertainties that can be reduced only by experience.

CHAPTER 10 *Summary*

This book began with the speculation that the theory of imperfect competition which forms so great a part of modern economics is capable of much simplification and at least a measure of substantive improvement; and that such a reconstructed theory of imperfect competition would, for certain purposes, constitute an acceptable substitute for the partial equilibrium theory of perfect competition. We ought now to consider how far these hopes have been realized. For convenience, we can organize our recapitulation under the headings of statics, dynamics, and policy lessons.

1 · STATICS. I submit that by adhering rigorously to the assumptions of static economic theory we have derived seven novel and significant results. For our purposes, the most important of these assumptions were:

(a) Entry into the imperfectly competitive industry is free in the sense that it will immediately take place whenever a new firm can establish itself without incurring a loss.

(b) All firms have equal access to resources and technology and therefore have the same production functions.

(c) All firms have complete freedom of contract, including freedom to merge, form profit-sharing cartels, and generally enter into side bargains.

(d) There is no uncertainty respecting demand for the industry's product or the resources and technology available to produce it.

(e) All firms are managed by profit maximizers.

1. On the above assumptions, the Robinson-Chamberlin type of tangency solution depicted in most treatments of imperfect competition was seen to be highly misleading. It purports to prove that imperfect competition gives rise to an equilibrium in which firms are of less than optimum size. Yet such an equilibrium of inefficiency can result only when restrictions are placed upon the right of firms to merge with one another, organize profit-sharing cartels, or otherwise cooperate in order to maximize profit; and such restrictions are ruled out by the postulate of static economic theory that gives complete freedom of contract to businessmen.

Given this freedom, the organization of any industry in which production is marked by technical inefficiency is inherently unstable. Firms that find themselves operating in such an industry will take two successive steps. They will first cooperate to organize production in the most efficient manner. (The legal form taken by this cooperation is unimportant to an economist.) They will then produce whatever output is necessary to force price low enough to discourage the entry of new firms. Given the existence of fixed cost in the plant, and a downward-sloping demand curve for the industry's product, there always exists a price which is high enough to yield the rationalized, multiplant enterprise that practices stay-out pricing a profit (or rent) but which is also low enough to make the entry of a new firm unprofitable.

We have found that, if the assumptions of static economic

theory are revised so as to place economically meaningful restrictions on mergers and cartels, an equilibrium with firms of less than optimum size will result. But we also saw that there is no unique equilibrium output for the industry in this case. More precisely, the equilibrium output that will result is a function of the set of restrictions imposed. When an imperfectly competitive industry consists of more than one firm, some assumption must be made about how the firms view their individual demand functions. And the view that each firm takes necessarily depends on how it believes rivals will react to its own price-output moves. Any number of views is possible. Each implies a different tangency solution for the individual firm and a different aggregate output for the industry.

Two of these tangency solutions were examined in detail. The first rested on postulates often employed by students of oligopoly that (a) a change in output by one firm will be matched by all other firms and (b) this fact is common knowledge in the industry. The second tangency solution rested on the venerable postulate taken from Cournot's treatment of duopoly. In altering its own output, a firm assumes that rival firms will not react by changing their outputs—and no firm ever discovers from experience that this assumption is wrong. Yet, although many tangency solutions are possible, every one requires the existence of some restriction on mergers and cartels in order to perpetuate itself. Therefore, in a world of free contract, every tangency solution is inherently unstable.

2. Our second result is closely related to the first. The distinction commonly drawn between perfect competition and imperfect competition was revealed as unimportant insofar as the allocation of resources is concerned. Given the existence of a fixed cost in the plant, competition is necessarily imperfect; and the amount of imperfection is wholly a function of the size of the most efficient plant relative to the demand for the

industry's product. Perfect competition can exist only when production, at every level of output, is carried on under constant returns to scale. In this case there is no fixed cost and hence no optimum size of the plant. All inputs are infinitely divisible; an industrial midget is as efficient as an industrial giant; no factor input can earn an economic rent; and, in equilibrium, price equals unit cost. Thus perfect competition, rigorously defined, is wholly a matter of technology and has nothing whatever to do with market organization.

If constant returns to scale do not prevail—if there is a fixed cost in the plant—then, in equilibrium, price will always exceed unit cost and the established firm (or firms) will earn economic rent. When the optimum size of the plant is very small relative to industry demand, when, for example, the industry can support 100 plants, it may be convenient to reason *as if* price is equal to unit cost in equilibrium. We have called this the case of proximate perfect competition. But such practice can only be justified as a pedagogical simplification. The important truth is that the existence of free entry in an industry will bring price and unit cost as close to equality as demand for the industry's product and the optimum size of the plant permit.

3. Our third notable result is a clear perception of the truth that the distinction between oligopoly and imperfect competition (and hence between oligopoly and perfect competition) is also unimportant insofar as resource allocation is concerned. This proposition is true at two levels. To say that, in imperfect competition, a firm "ignores" the possible reactions of its rivals to its own output changes is only to say that it regards the "unused" portion of the industry's demand curve as its own. This is the assumption on which Cournot long ago built his analysis of duopoly—the simplest form of oligopoly. In this sense imperfect competition is only one form of oligopoly.

However, there is a more important way in which the distinction between oligopoly and imperfect competition is unimportant. As we have seen, in static economic theory, the uncoordinated rivalry of several firms cannot produce a stable equilibrium. In the short run such rivalry may produce a tangency solution, but in the long run the firms will join together to rationalize production and practice the stay-out pricing needed to discourage potential entrants. When this happens, their rivalry perforce ceases to be uncoordinated.

4. Our reconstruction of the theory of imperfect competition extended it to embrace the whole phenomenon of "economic rationalization" that has been slighted in static economic theory. In an economic model that assumes freedom of contract, mergers, cartels, spin-offs, subcontracting, and other side bargains are the usual methods by which firms cooperate to maximize profit. Yet these devices are commonly treated in economic theory (when they are treated at all) as the tools of "monopoly." In reality, there is no important difference between the problem of organizing a profit-sharing cartel and the problem of organizing a multiplant firm. To neglect the process by which rival businessmen cooperate to rationalize economic activity is to neglect an important part of their behavior. Nor can we justify the disregard of this process by objecting that the American economy has long operated in a legal framework which makes cartels illegal. Cartels, after all, have imperfect substitutes—mergers, the mental telepathy that is apparent in price leadership, market sharing, and the division of output and profit within an industry through subcontracting.

By giving an honorable place to the techniques of economic rationalization, our revised theory of imperfect competition also provides a more coherent view of the connection between equilibrium of the firm and equilibrium of the industry than was previously available. It reveals that, in static economic theory, one equilibrium implies the other and, indeed, that they are simultaneously determined.

5. Our venture in revisionism has described a technique that may allow economists more efficiently to explain the essentials of static economic theory to beginning students. It is not really necessary to introduce the sophomores to static economic theory by taxing their powers of abstraction with the need to assume that an industry is composed of a very large number of producers of the same product, none of whom has the power to affect the price of what he produces. Sophomores *know* that, in the real world, an "industry" is typically composed of a relatively small number of firms which produce differentiated products and whose managers are perfectly aware that their decisions *do* influence price. A presentation which assumes from the start that, in equilibrium, the industry can consist of a single firm with several plants will surely encounter less consumer resistance than the usual textbook exposition of perfect competition.

Chapter 4 concluded that, as long as there was constant unit cost in the industry for multiples of the optimum output of the optimum size plant, then the industry would be organized as a rationalized enterprise, as one big firm or one big cartel. The beginning student in economics may, at first, have some difficulty in following the progression of arguments by which we reach this conclusion. He will not find any of them unreasonable *per se*. Rather, the danger is that our reconstruction of the theory of imperfect competition caters too much to the prejudices of the beginning student—or at any rate to those of the campus sophisticate who, having made the acquaintance of J. K. Galbraith, assumes, as a matter of course, that the economy is dominated by "big business."

6. Our reconstruction has delivered another blow for credi-

bility in economics. It allows a place for the sense of rivalry which has been allowed to linger in static economic theory only in brief discussions of oligopoly. In the models of this book every price-output decision is made with the conscious intent to exclude rivals from the industry. When entry into an industry is wholly free, nobody will, in fact, enter since a firm which secures control of the industry will maximize its long-run profit first by setting a price that is low enough to discourage entry of any other firm. When entry is impeded, the established firm may elect to gamble by charging more than a stay-out price that minimizes the risk of entry. In both cases, however, the firm has a price-output policy which takes account of the existence of actual or potential rivals.

7. Finally, we found in Chapter 5 that our reconstructed theory of imperfect competition could easily be extended to cover the case of an industry which produces differentiated products. When this step is taken, the multiplant firm becomes the multiproduct firm, but nothing else is changed. In equilibrium the industry is organized as a single enterprise which practices stay-out pricing; production is carried on in the most efficient manner; and the divergence between price and long-run marginal cost for every variety of the product produced is due entirely to the existence of fixed cost in the plant. The intervention of a Central Planning Commission to close this gap could cause the amount of product variety in the industry to rise, fall, or remain unchanged. The actual outcome would depend upon the nature of the costs that must be incurred to differentiate the basic product.

That some of the product variety of the real world is "bad" was accepted as obviously and tritely true. (We can make the same point about some of the product standardization of the real world.) The condemnation of any particular instance of product differentiation, however, necessarily involves a judgment about producer morals and/or consumer competence and so carried us beyond the proper jurisdiction of static economic theory.

2 · DYNAMICS. Chapters 6 through 9 considered a few of the results which follow from relaxing the assumption that production is carried on in an imperfectly competitive industry under conditions of perfect certainty. In Chapters 6 and 7 we found that, when perfect certainty is ruled out, entry into the industry becomes "impeded"; that stationary equilibrium with an unchanging output over time is no longer possible for the industry; and that an outbreak of economic warfare is an ever-present possibility. That is, when an established firm is faced with the imminent entry of a rival, it may seek to destroy him by a price war. We attached importance to this conclusion because recent research has implied that economic warfare is somehow "irrational." In fact, economic warfare as a logical possibility can be excluded only when the assumption of perfect certainty is made. In the strictly static case, if monopoly is a feasible goal for the industry, it can be more cheaply obtained through a merger or cartel than through a price war.

In Chapters 8 and 9 we considered, if only briefly, the role of information in the theory of imperfect competition. We found that, once businessmen are presumed to make their decisions on the basis of incomplete information, they cannot be said to "maximize profit." They are presented with alternative uses for the resources which they command and the opportunity to discover additional alternative uses by employing part of their resources to search for additional information. The decision rules which they use to determine resource allocation depend partly upon their attitudes toward uncertainty and partly upon the cost of acquiring additional information. There is no reason to believe that all businessmen in "objectively" similar circumstances will elect to base their operations upon the same decision rules.

3 · POLICY LESSONS. Finally, we turn to the implications of our study for public policy toward competition. They are, to put it mildly, unsettling. The most general conclusion is that static economic theory cannot be used to "prove" the desirability of legal rules that restrict freedom of contract in the interest of "promoting competition." On the contrary, static economic theory can be used to establish a presumption that most rules of this sort will reduce economic welfare.

A legal rule which limits the use of mergers or cartels in an imperfectly competitive industry (while entry remains free) will *ceteris paribus* condemn it to technically inefficient production. More precisely, control of mergers and cartels condemns the imperfectly competitive industry to some type of tangency solution wherein every plant produces too small an output. Furthermore, controls on mergers and cartels may actually lead to a smaller industry output than would result if the industry were allowed to pass into the hands of a single producer. This is true even though the single big producer enjoys no economies of scale not available to smaller firms. Likewise, the use of the trust-busting power to convert a so-called monopoly—an industry consisting of only one producer—into an oligopoly can serve to make the industry less efficient whenever demand is subject to seasonal or cyclical variation (Chapter 3).

The most that we can say for antitrust is that, whenever a restriction on the use of mergers or cartels will produce a greater equilibrium output than would a policy of laissez-faire, it is *possible* that economic welfare will be increased by constraining freedom of contract. This possibility will perforce be realized if the welfare gain from the increase in output is greater than the welfare loss resulting from the reduction in technical efficiency.

When we turn to the merits of restrictions on freedom of contract under conditions of uncertainty, we can afford some, but not much more, comfort to friends of antitrust. Here our principal finding was that, insofar as competition is a search for information, it must "break down" as the desired information is acquired and put to use. It follows, of course, that this transformation from search phase to static phase in the firm can be retarded by the adoption of legal rules designed to frustrate learning. Thus variations in price, changes in product design, and price wars among rival firms can be encouraged by the severe enforcement of antitrust rules that make it a penitentiary offense for businessmen to exchange market information. Whether the economic benefits gained from such a policy outweigh the economic losses should strike economists as very doubtful.

Our usual presumption is that, since most people have an aversion to most types of economic uncertainty, any development that reduces economic uncertainty *pari passu* increases economic welfare. Our discussion of uncertainty and imperfect competition also stressed that uncertainty encourages the persistence of competition defined as "many firms." If the policy goal is to preserve some minimum number of firms in an industry, this end can be advanced by making it impossible for rival businessmen to gain the information that would lead them to place their firms under unified central management. Yet, here again, we are condemned to the indignity of stating the obvious. Whatever the benefits of decentralized decision making, a policy that perpetuates it by preserving ignorance has an economic cost.

Sophisticated friends of antitrust policy, especially in economics, have long been reluctant to argue that the competition peculiar to the multifirm industry is worth preserving and promoting even at the cost of reducing economic welfare. This reluctance arises from an understandable but nevertheless unfortunate wish to be thought "tough-minded." It reflects a fear that any case for antitrust policy which does not rest on arguments that antitrust actually increases economic welfare will be dismissed by one's audience as "romantic" or "unscientific." My own feeling is that the unwillingness to make use of the non-economic arguments for antitrust policy is misguided. The economic costs of antitrust are much more easily identified and measured than its economic benefits. Thus "everybody knows" that the merger of the Pennsylvania and New York Central railroads allows a more intelligent use of railroad resources that range from cost accountants to switch engines, whereas the loss in economic welfare that results because a certain amount of competition is eliminated between the two carriers is quite nebulous. Given the difficulty, if not the impossibility, of constructing an economic case for antitrust, the conclusion is unavoidable. No intellectually respectable argument for antitrust can be advanced that does not rest squarely on the value judgment that some amount of economic welfare ought to be sacrificed to ensure some amount of intra-industry competition.

One need not assert that the preservation of some minimum amount of intra-industry competition is a good thing *per se*. Its protection may be viewed as necessary in order to preserve small business as a "way of life" or to foster the mental attitudes that will make possible the survival of some approved form of capitalism. In the same spirit the managers of a socialist economy which permits some private trade in the retail and service sectors may limit the size of private firms, and so reduce efficiency, in order to prevent the reemergence of an influential "big" bourgeoisie. The task of economists is not to defend the claims of economic welfare against alternative social goals—even though we often do play this role because we discover that nobody else will. But it does fall to our lot, East and West, to make clear that the pursuit of these alternatives can—and usually does—involve a sacrifice of economic welfare.

Index of Authors

Index of Subjects